Become a member o
community:

Sign up for Reiner's newsletter
- *reinerlomb.com/news/subscribe*

Connect with Reiner on social media
- LinkedIn: *ReinerLomb*
- Twitter: *@ReinerLomb*

Share ASPIRE with others
- To order copies of ASPIRE go to: *reinerlomb.com/books*

Contact Reiner
- To ask about Reiner's availability for speaking, coaching or workshops go to: *reinerlomb.com/contact*

Praise for *ASPIRE:*
Seven Essential Emotions for Leading Positive Change, No Matter Where You Are

"I have often said that effective servant leadership is an inside job—a question of the heart. Reiner Lomb's book *ASPIRE*, and the leadership model it is named for, addresses this question beautifully. Read this book and discover, analyze and apply Lomb's seven essential leadership behaviors and emotions for creating positive change. When you do, it will unleash your servant's heart and inspire you to lead at a higher level."

Ken Blanchard – Coauthor of *The New One Minute Manager*® and *Simple Truths of Leadership: 52 Ways to Be a Servant Leader and Build Trust*

"This book goes way beyond the typical leadership advice. Author Reiner Lomb writes that great leaders need to have a strong handle on their emotions as drivers of leadership behavior. From Lomb's experience as a top executive coach, the reader learns a well-constructed, sequential and eminently practical process called ASPIRE. This book will help leaders become more aware of their emotional states and show them how to inspire others and create needed change."

Jennifer B. Kahnweiler, Ph.D. – Author of *Creating Introvert-Friendly Workplaces* and *The Introverted Leader*

"This book makes a huge claim. No matter who you are, you can create positive change in the world. Few people believe this, so few people do it. This book is a must-read for those who yearn to make a difference."

Robert E. Quinn – Professor at University of Michigan Center for Positive Leadership and author of *Deep Change, Discovering the Leader Within*

"What a delight. I truly enjoyed reading this book and love Reiner's work. He is a master at unpacking the complexity of the human experience. His approach simplifies the dynamics of emotions and behavior and provides realistic actionable steps and disciplines to live life intentionally every day. Reiner's personal story and those of his clients provide the canvas to see his approach in action. If your desire is to earn the reputation of being a difference maker, *ASPIRE* is a companion for your journey to the future."

Nancy M. Dahl – Board Director, CEO and award-winning author of *Grounded – Leading your life with intention.*

"*ASPIRE* is an excellent book. The emotional competencies shared by Reiner Lomb introduced me to a new and provocative perspective for leadership. Practicing these leadership emotions helps me make the dynamic shift to support a bold vision. Practicing emotional competencies gives me the energy for the essential behaviors to lead change and be a better person. I highly recommend *ASPIRE* to anyone passionate about leading change."

Dr. Bennie L. Harris – Chancellor, University of South Carolina Upstate

"Reiner Lomb, in his latest book, *ASPIRE*, offers leaders a new approach to leading change: managing our own emotions to accomplish the behaviors we desire. He uses true and fascinating examples from world leaders changing the course of history to his own coaching clients impacting their teams' success. I especially appreciated how Lomb focuses on simple and critical emotions, like Trust, yet acknowledges the complexity of achieving it by elaboration: it includes 'Trust IN you as a leader. Trust BY you in your stakeholders. And Trust BETWEEN your stakeholders.' Throughout this book, leaders will gain both insight and the ability to lead even more effectively."

Martha Legare – Executive Coach and CEO, The Gantt Group

"Reiner Lomb clearly and succinctly understands what good leadership is and how to develop the emotional stances that make leaders great. *ASPIRE* is a very well written book, rare among business literature these days, which makes it easier to learn how to build the emotional energy that is the root cause of great leadership. *ASPIRE* shows that there are seven emotions that lead naturally to great leadership behaviors and leadership presence. As I read I could feel a shift to a more positive state of mind. As I did the very practical exercises that develop the ability to manifest each of the seven emotions critical to effective leadership, I felt a deeper and more permanent transformation. I am spending more time in the emotions that make the world and the organization better and less time in those that keep me and those I lead from achieving our potential. This book can help you to become a better leader by developing your capacity to live in the emotions that are the root causes of effective leadership. You will enjoy the low stress feeling of leadership coming naturally from a well-developed heart."

Gifford Pinchot III – Entrepreneur, President of Pinchot & Company and Author of *Intrapreneuring*

"Reiner's *ASPIRE* masterfully links the power of emotional self-awareness to being an effective, influential leader. Just as a car 'shifts' to a different gear in response to driving conditions, so can everyone (we are all leaders) control our own emotional states and responses. By 'shifting' to the desired emotion, we 'drive' our behaviors, which are conducive to influencing others in fostering meaningful change. This ability is foundational in supporting Reiner's premise that 'a leader aspires to create positive, aspirational change.'"

Bret Lessman – Former senior executive in organizational development with international organizations, including Hewlett-Packard and Siemens AG

"As Reiner Lomb eloquently articulates in *ASPIRE*, the day of emotions-centered leadership has arrived. Emotions drive your actions and those of your team. They determine what you say and how you say it. Everything you do as a leader is influenced by emotions. Emotional competence is no longer a nice-to-have for leaders. Reading this book will give you a practical understanding of how you can immediately begin leveraging emotions for greater effectiveness. You'll be grateful you took the time. I highly recommend it!"

Dan Newby – Author of *The Field Guide to Emotions* and founder of The School of Emotions

"I couldn't agree more with Reiner Lomb. *ASPIRE* is essential for the leaders of our time. The organizations and institutions that have the power to change the world are run by emotional beings. Fear, resentment, anger and distrust keep us from collaborating on the big challenges of our time. *ASPIRE* offers leaders and changemakers the essential emotional competencies to change that. I highly recommend this book to anyone who is passionate about creating positive change."

Klaus Moegling, Ph.D. – Associate professor, teacher trainer and author of *Realignment. A Peaceful and Sustainably Developed World Is (Still) Possible*

"In *ASPIRE*, Reiner Lomb identifies seven essential emotions that drive seven key leadership behaviors. Lomb brings these emotions and behaviors to life with engaging stories and examples from his own work as a coach, giving readers a clear understanding of how they can be put into practice and the benefits for doing so."

Charles Feltman – Executive coach and author *The Thin Book of Trust: An Essential Primer for Building Trust at Work*

"Successful organizational change is dependent on how the leader shows up. The seven essential emotions shared by Reiner Lomb in his thought-provoking book provide the reader with important leadership qualities that, when practiced, lead to positive organizational change. Before starting your change journey, read this book."

Richard Axelrod – Author of *Terms of Engagement: New Ways to Lead and Change Organizations*

DEDICATION

For Remi.

*May emotions for positive change be companions on your
journey to the future.*

CONTENTS

ACKNOWLEDGEMENTS

The challenge of writing a book is often compared with giving birth to a baby. While I cannot truly speak to the inner experience of a mother giving birth, I can speak to my inner experience of writing this book. There were times when I was optimistic and enthusiastic, but there were also times when I was not sure if I wanted to continue because I felt stuck. As readers can see in Chapter 7: Positivity – Being Resilient, my practice of what I share there helped me overcome those roadblocks. But another valued resource were the people who supported me at various stages in the process. I would like to express my deepest gratitude and thanks to the following people. My intention is to pay your kindness forward.

Robert E. Quinn, whose teaching and mentorship has greatly shaped my learning in the field of leadership, gave me invaluable feedback about my approach, the ASPIRE Leadership Model, and its application with *The Competing Values Framework,* which he and John Rohrbaugh originally developed (see Appendix).

Ken Blanchard's questions and advice helped me rethink my approach to my reader's needs. He also supported my application of the ASPIRE Leadership Model with the *SLII® Model* that he developed (see Appendix).

Phyllis Ring supported me graciously by sharing her expertise as an accomplished author, reviewing the chapters as I was developing them and, most importantly, providing emotional support throughout the whole process.

Donna Kozik and team, who had already helped me edit and publish my first book, *The Boomerang Approach,* edited the manuscript and helped me with publishing.

Leona Stahlmann, who is part of a new generation of rising German authors, provided me with some important fresh perspective on the manuscript.

The conversations with my colleague, Udaiyan Jatar (U.J.), and the many client projects and teachings we have collaborated on together inspired me to develop the ASPIRE Leadership Model and apply it to the *Blue Earth Model* © for innovation that he created (see Appendix).

Bret Lessman, Augusta Nash and Guenther Stahlmann were test readers of early versions of the manuscript as well as Greg Camenzind, who also supported the digital marketing activities of the launch.

Dick and Emily Axelrod, Steve Piersanti, Jennifer Kahnweiler and Nancy Dahl each gave me important advice on my publishing and marketing path.

My wife, Marienne Bernardes, was always there for me when I needed to bounce off ideas or, even more importantly, needed encouragement. My children, Maximilian and Sofia were always checking in and it reminded me why I was writing ASPIRE.

I'm also grateful for the inspiration and learning that the works of the following people have provided me. I am thankful to stand on their shoulders. This list of those whose work has taught and inspired me is by no means complete: Abraham Maslow, Viktor Frankl, Stephen Covey, Peter Drucker, Robert Greenleaf, Karen Armstrong, Martin Seligman, Gisela Oettingen, Charles Feltman, Barbara Frederickson, Dan Newby and Lucy Nuñez, Julio Olalla, Rafael Echeverría, Joseph Grenny, Daniel Goleman, Lisa Feldman Barrett, Paul Gilbert, Choden, Dacher Keltner, Lou Salomon, Kristin Neff, Paul J. Silvia, Ann K. Renninger and Suzanne E. Hidi, John Zenger and Joseph Folkman, Paul J. Zak, Phil Sandahl and Alexis Phillips, Gifford and Libba Pinchot, Brene Brown and others. References to some of their works can be found in the bibliography section.

Last but not least, I am thankful for the many people whose stories I have shared here anonymously and particularly those who gave me permission to use their real names, including Anke Jahn, who shared the story of her escape from East Germany; Chairman Manuel Heart of the Ute Mountain Ute Tribe; Traci Snowden, founder and CEO of Apto Global; Srinivas Yamujala, global technology executive; and Klaus Moegling, author and activist.

"Many small people, who in many small places do many small things, can alter the face of the world."

~ East Side Gallery, Berlin Wall Memorial

PREFACE:
The Intangible Force

Many of my own experiences have inspired the creation of The ASPIRE Leadership Model. Yet one stands out above all others as an illustration of the power of emotions in leading change. Let's travel back to the time and place of that experience.

The Fall of the Wall

It's November 9, 1989, and I am on vacation in Cuba. It is already late and I'm trying to sleep, but the sound of cheering outside my hotel room keeps me awake.

I get up and open the door to ask the noisemakers to be quiet, but before I'm able to speak, a man shouts at me, "Die Mauer ist gefallen!" ("The Wall came down!")

I shake my head, thinking, "How drunk must he be that he believes the Wall has come down?" I go back to bed, not believing what I have heard.

Living with the Wall

I grew up in West Germany only 20 miles from the border to East Germany. That border was part of the "Iron Curtain," a 4,562-mile barrier of fences, walls, minefields and watchtowers that divided Europe all the way from Norway in the north to the Black Sea in the south. The Berlin Wall that was part of this physical barrier had been built in 1961, when I was 5 years old, to stop the exodus from the East.

The border ran through our local mountains. I would hike there with my friends along the heavily guarded double fence, watching the East German guards in their towers as they watched us. The space between the double fence was called "Der Todesstreifen" (the death strip). The East German guards were under orders to shoot anyone trying to flee across the border.

West German television often showed images of wounded or dead bodies being carried away by East German guards. While I could speak up freely on my side of the border, my cousin Heinz on the other side could not. Shortly after his high school graduation in the fall of 1950, Heinz had gathered a group of friends at his home where they discussed the latest change in voting rights by the East German government. They saw this change as a threat to freedom and democracy and discussed printing and distributing leaflets to inform people about their concern.

Yet they never acted on this, and all moved on to their next phase in life. Nearly two years had passed when one night police showed up at Heinz's door and, under a false pretense, abducted and handed him over to the Soviet Secret Service (MGB). His friends were abducted in a similar way. Someone had disclosed their names and information about their meeting. In a secret process by a military court, Heinz and three of his friends were convicted for planning acts of terrorism and sentenced to death, while the others were sentenced to 25 years in the Gulag.

On October 23, 1952, the day before his 21st birthday, Heinz was led out of his cell and into the execution room at the notorious Butyrka Prison in Moscow. He was executed with a gunshot to the back of his head. His body was unceremoniously cremated, and his ashes, together with those of many others, were scattered at Donskoje Cemetery in Moscow.

The Intangible Barriers

The area of my hometown of Fulda was named the "Fulda Gap" by the U.S. military because the topographical conditions offered a gap for the Soviet Union to enter West Germany with their tanks and draw a wedge into NATO territory. If such an attack were to occur, an American nuclear response was a very real possibility. If World War III were to happen between the countries of the Warsaw Pact and NATO, it was predicted that it would start there. Thinking how close we were to such a horrific scenario at that time still sends chills down my spine.

Although our West German leaders tried to keep the hope of reunification alive, it seemed unlikely. The turmoil of the times made it hard for me to see such a future as possible, especially given the control that the East German regime held over its people and the control and power the Soviet Union had over the East German regime.

Seeing these insurmountable barriers—the Iron Curtain and the nuclear weapons that threatened to destroy us—and lacking historical perspective at my young age, a peaceful revolution that would bring down the Wall was beyond my imagination. I lacked optimism and so was unable to envision a different future. Emotions predispose us to action or inaction. In the same way that my lack of optimism was a barrier to envisioning a future without the Wall, fear and hopelessness were the intangible barriers for the majority of East Germans. These kept them from taking collective and coordinated action to demand what they aspired to: freedom and democracy. Overcoming those barriers required an emotional shift.

In the summer of 1989, only weeks before the Wall came down, thousands of East Germans were still fleeing to the West because they had no hope that things would change within their country. Anke Jahn, a friend of mine and 18-year-old Leipzig resident at that time, described it like this: "The mood in our city was still very depressed and pessimistic. Although, like many of my friends,

I was wearing a Gorbachev button—a symbol of change—on my jacket, I had no hope that things would actually change."

While she was pessimistic that things could change for her country as a whole, one day she had a sudden inner shift to optimism that if she tried to escape, she would be successful. Without sharing her real intentions with her parents and siblings, she left on July 31 with a friend to go on a camping trip to Hungary. They stayed there at a campground near the border to Yugoslavia, hoping that one of the trucks that passed by would smuggle them across the border. They went every day and waited at the side of the road. After two weeks of waiting, a West German truck driver who was on his way to Greece agreed to take them.

That night, he picked them up, hid them under a tarpaulin in the back of the truck, and then they were taken to the Hungarian-Yugoslavian border. At the border, the truck rolled to a stop, and they heard the voices of the border guards. Anke and her friend held their breath while the guards inspected the vehicle with their flashlights.

"The guards' faces were so close to our faces that we were afraid they would hear us breathing," Anke remembered. They were not discovered, but they still had a long ride to Greece. After another day and night, they safely crossed the border to Greece and went straight to the West German Consulate. Now they were free.

Anke later told me that she had made the risky decision because she wanted nothing more than being free to travel and elect a government that would give her hope for the future. She was not at all optimistic that the East German Regime would ever fulfill the demand of its citizens for free travel and free elections.

Emotions – The Intangible Force for Change

At the end of the summer in 1989, the mood suddenly shifted among the people in East Germany. A seed of hope and optimism that freedom and democracy were possible—the same vision my cousin Heinz had died for and Anke pursued—was planted in Leipzig with a small group of people who attended what was later called the Monday Demonstrations. These occurred on September 4, 1989, after the Monday Peace Prayer that was regularly held in the nearby Nicolaikirche. These peaceful demonstrations then continued Monday after Monday with a rapidly growing number of people coming to demonstrate.

Organizing and attending the peace prayers and demonstrations took courage. Christian Fuehrer and Christoph Wonneberg, the two young pastors who hosted and helped organize the Monday prayers, had become targets of intense secret police surveillance and pressure, and peaceful demonstrators were brutally beaten and jailed. Despite these intimidating attempts to suppress the voice of the people, participation in the Monday Demonstrations grew week after week to 70,000, 120,000 and then 320,000 by October 23, the day when—in a city of 500,000—more people were marching in the streets than were watching from their windows. People in other cities followed suit, and millions across the country went to the streets.

A crucial moment came on the evening of November 9, 1989, when Guenther Schabowski, an East German government official, announced to a group of press representatives that the border would immediately be open for East Germans with a valid passport. Only a few miles away from the Internal Press Center in East Berlin, where the announcement was made, 46-year-old Harald Jaeger, the highest-ranking border guard at the Bornholmer Strasse border crossing at the Berlin Wall that night, was just taking the first bite of his dinner sandwich when he heard the announcement on the cafeteria TV in his workplace. He never finished eating his sandwich. Instead, he immediately called his supervisor, Colonel Rudi Ziegenhorn, to ask for orders on how to deal with the situation. Ziegenhorn dismissed the announcement by Schabowski and gave Jaeger the order not to open the border.

East Germans living near the Wall had also heard Schabowski's announcement on their TVs and left their homes to come to the border crossing that Jaeger and his colleagues were guarding. As they watched the crowd grow bigger and shout, "Open the gate!" Jaeger's colleagues urged him to get out the machine guns. Jaeger rejected that idea, but kept calling his supervisor for orders, only to be threatened that he would have to bear the consequences if he disobeyed and opened the gate. This was a serious threat to a man who had been a loyal Stasi member for 28 years and had a wife and children. He felt deserted by his superiors and disappointed that his colleagues were not on his side. After hours of inner struggle, Harald Jaeger commanded his guards to open the gate and let people pass. Border guards at other border crossings followed, and around the world people watched television images of the people in Berlin streaming across the border and ecstatically celebrating their freedom.

When Harald Jaeger was asked about his decision years later, he demurred in taking credit for bringing down the Wall and instead acknowledged those who had rallied in the streets for their freedom and democracy. Millions, paralyzed for decades by fear, hopelessness and distrust, had found optimism and courage, the intangible force that mobilized them to bring down the insurmountable physical barrier: the Berlin Wall.

Why We Need to Change the Way We Lead

I grew up in Germany, a country that was divided by a physical barrier. Yet, more than 30 years after the fall of the Wall, I live in the United States, so I am again in a country that is divided. Yet looking beyond the United States, other countries and the world in general are divided too.

What divides us today is not a wall made of bricks, but one made of emotions. Fear, resentment, anger and distrust divide us from others and keep us from collaborating with each other. Yet challenges that threaten our future and the future of our children, such as climate change, pandemics, economic, social, racial and health inequalities, mass migration and others require us to overcome the division so we can work together.

That is why we need to change the way we lead. That means changing our leadership behaviors. Yet changing our behaviors is often not so easy because of intangible barriers—our emotions. Research in emotional psychology suggests there is no action you take that is not affected by your emotions. Emotions drive behavior.

The good news is that emotions can be learned, meaning you can become aware of and shift your emotions and, with that, your leadership behavior. Yes, that's right—you can learn to change your emotions. The question is, which emotions are the most important to learn, and how can you learn them?

The following introduction provides an overview of the seven essential emotions that drive the leadership behaviors that will enable you to create positive change.

"Over the years, I have become a strong believer in the fact that the external world can be changed by altering our internal world."
~ Robert E. Quinn

INTRODUCTION:
The ASPIRE Leadership Model

The essence of leadership is creating a vision of an aspirational new future and then influencing people to change their behavior to make that vision a reality.

Your inspiration to create aspirational change may come from your dissatisfaction with the status quo, joyful anticipation of an aspirational new future or a new insight. In the example of the peaceful revolution in East Germany, all three factors were at play. The East Germans who went to the streets were dissatisfied with the lack of democracy and freedom; they were looking forward to traveling freely, and their new insight was that through the rise of Gorbachev as the new Soviet leader, change was possible.

This created an emotional shift from hopelessness to optimism and to inspiration, which mobilized millions of East Germans to act, despite fear of police violence. It was that emotional shift that changed their behavior from inaction to action that created the freedom they aspired to.

As a leader, you can create such an emotional shift in yourself to drive the right leadership behavior so that you can influence others to change their behavior to make your vision a reality.

Let's look in more detail at how emotions affect leadership behavior.

How Emotions Affect Behavior

While there is no consensus on a single definition of emotions, there is consensus that they affect our behavior. For practical reasons, I suggest the definition offered by Dan Newby and Lucy Nuñez in their primer in emotional literacy that says an emotion is that which puts us in motion.

This means emotions are an energy that drives our behavior or, in the context of this book, our leadership behavior.

Many people still hold the long-standing belief that emotions are automatic, universal and hardwired in different regions of our brain, and therefore they are just happening to us. Psychologist and neuroscientist Lisa Feldman Barrett overturns this belief based on her groundbreaking research on emotions.

Her findings show that our brain constructs emotions by continually predicting and simulating all the sensory information from inside and outside our bodies, so it understands what this information means and what to do about it. That means that we are responsible for our emotions and moods, and we can learn to become aware of our emotional state. If we find that it's not useful for our desired leadership behavior, we can then shift it to the emotional state that drives our desired behavior.

Shifting to the desired emotion does not mean avoiding certain other emotions. Each emotion has its purpose. For example, feeling fear may notify us about a potential danger as a predisposition to taking an action that protects us, such as running away or defending ourselves. Feeling grief may predispose us to a search for meaning when we have lost someone or something.

The challenge is when an emotion is not fulfilling its purpose, such as feeling fear when there is no real danger, which keeps us from taking action toward an important goal or taking the wrong action. Shifting to an emotion that supports a desired leadership behavior requires becoming aware of what we're feeling and assessing whether that emotion is helpful in this moment and if not, to shift to the emotion that is helpful.

You are always in an emotional state, whether you are aware of it or not, and it is usually a mixture of different emotions. It's this mixture that drives your behavior, and it may or may not support the leadership behavior you need at that moment to achieve your goal.

To create an inspiring vision, mobilize your team or coordinate effective actions, you need the kind of positive emotions that help motivate these outcomes. That's why becoming aware of your emotions and learning to shift to the emotions that support your desired leadership behavior is such a critical leadership skill.

While in everyday language we often use the terms "emotions" and "moods" interchangeably, psychologists actually make a distinction. An emotion is more intense and short-lived, such as when we are angry because someone cut us off in traffic. A mood is an emotional state that is usually milder but longer-lasting, such as an ongoing anxiety we may feel during an extended crisis like a pandemic.

A useful model to create emotional awareness and mastery in the context of behavior is to think of emotions as drivers of or barriers to the desired leadership behavior. This means that the ability to understand your own emotional barriers and drivers and those of the other person is essential for changing your own behavior and influencing a change in the behavior of others.

The effect of emotions on behaviors is at the core of the ASPIRE Leadership Model. The model consists of seven essential leadership behaviors for creating aspirational change and the seven emotions that drive those behaviors. Learning the seven essential emotions and how to shift to the ones you need will drive the leadership behaviors that help you create the change you aspire to, no matter where you are.

Here is a brief overview of each of the seven leadership behaviors and associated emotions of the ASPIRE Leadership Model that will be covered in detail in Chapters 1–7.

Seven Essential Leadership Behaviors and Emotions

Chapter 1: Empathy – The Gate to Caring

The first leadership behavior is *caring*. The leader who doesn't appear to care about the people she is leading is not trusted by them, and if a leader is not trusted, people don't follow her. That is why it is not a surprise that caring leaders and their organizations have greater engagement of their employees, perform better than their competitors and attract more talent than those that don't have a caring culture. In a caring culture, people show a genuine concern for and interest in the well-being of others, and leaders play an essential role modeling those behaviors. Unfortunately, I have seen many cases where people in a leadership role don't show care about the needs of their stakeholders. But a person can learn to care.

Caring about another person can be aroused by feeling *emotional empathy* for that person or group of people. Emotional empathy is an emotional resonance with what another person feels. When a friend is grieving the loss of her mother and you feel sadness about your friend's loss—or may even be grieving the loss of your friend's mom yourself—that sadness or grief makes you care about your friend and her suffering. Caring and its emotional driver, emotional empathy, are so fundamental to leadership that they provide the foundation for all other leadership competencies of the ASPIRE Leadership Model.

Chapter 2: Compassion – The Commitment to Serving

The second leadership behavior is *serving*. It builds on caring about someone's needs, but in addition, we act on our caring. In the example of the friend who is grieving the loss of her mother, going from caring to serving means taking action to support her in some way.

Great leaders are committed to serve. The question is, what emotion does one need to feel that drives that commitment? Compassion is the emotion that drives one to commit to serving the needs of another person or group of people. In the case of the friend who just lost her mother, while emotional empathy makes one feel the friend's emotion and that makes one care, it is compassion that commits one to act. Examples of this include staying with the grieving friend and looking for ways to ease her suffering, such as comforting her in her pain and taking care of responsibilities she is not able to do herself, such as preparing meals.

Chapter 3: Interest – The Drive to Understanding

Trying to understand before we act is important advice for anyone, but it's absolutely critical for a leader because of the impact a leader's decisions have on a team, organization or society. It is also essential for a leader to truly develop an understanding of their stakeholders' needs, circumstances and what would meet their needs. Such understanding enables a leader to influence her stakeholders positively, not to manipulate, but to serve their needs. For example, a leader who understands the career aspirations of a team member is able to support him more effectively in his career development, which will inspire the team member to give his best.

Interest is the key to gaining this understanding. It is the emotion that can be described as a state in which you are pulled to explore and to immerse yourself in what you are discovering. Interest in understanding another person builds on empathy and compassion. This motivates you to seek out opportunities to put yourself into the other person's shoes and be motivated and committed to serve her needs.

Chapter 4: Optimism – The Lens for Visioning

The fourth essential behavior of a leader, after caring, serving and understanding, is the ability to envision an aspirational new future for her stakeholders. When an organization has a vision that meets its employees' highest aspirations, it provides a common purpose that pulls everybody forward. A similar pull could be observed with the East Germans who were drawn to demonstrate in the streets for their freedom and democracy. That vision generated a deep and sustained commitment to act, as demonstrated by the people in Leipzig who showed up Monday after Monday to make their feelings and aspirations known.

Yet many leaders struggle to create a truly inspiring vision. They are often held back by the day-to-day challenges or past failures that put them in an emotional state that blocks them from thinking about the future. Creating a positive vision requires leaders to be in an emotional state of *optimism*. Optimism allows them to focus on the future.

We can find plenty of examples in history where even though change seemed to be impossible at the time, leaders emerged who were able to express an aspirational vision of the future. Their optimism enabled them to have that vision. Examples include the Civil Rights Movement led by Martin Luther King Jr. that achieved the Voting Rights Act in the U.S. and South Africa's Anti-Apartheid Movement led by Nelson Mandela in the 1980s, which led to a democratic society in which citizens of all races are allowed to vote.

Chapter 4 will show you how to develop optimism and apply it to your own day-to-day leadership challenges.

Chapter 5: Inspiration – The Energy for Mobilizing

The previous section emphasized the importance for a leader of envisioning an aspirational new future. Making that vision a reality requires action. Without it, it is merely daydreaming. That's why mobilizing stakeholders to act toward the vision is critical. Mobilizing is the fifth of the seven essential leadership behaviors.

In the same way that emotions fuel the previous four leadership behaviors, inspiration is the emotion that mobilizes people to act. For some, inspiring others comes naturally. However, for many it is challenging. Having a vision that aligns with people's aspirations provides the foundation for inspiring people. Yet, there are also leadership behaviors that can be a barrier to inspiration, such as lack of caring, while others can be inspiring, such as connecting the vision to people's aspirations.

Chapter 5 will provide more insights into behaviors that are barriers to inspiration and those that help to inspire.

Chapter 6: Trust – The Fuel for Collaborating

Once a leader has mobilized the right people to support the vision, the sixth essential leadership behavior is to coordinate effective actions. This can be done by setting measurable goals, creating action plans and assigning roles and responsibilities for executing plans. This is as true for executing toward a vision of societal change, like freedom and democracy, as it is for an organizational change, like creating a new business. In the example of the East German revolution, after people were mobilized, it was time to coordinate actions, which required effective collaboration among them.

Trust is the emotion that fuels collaboration among people. When you trust, you make yourself or something you value vulnerable to another person's actions. It is one of the more complex emotions.

Chapter 6 will explore the different dimensions of trust and how they can be developed.

Chapter 7: Positivity – Being Resilient

The seventh leadership behavior is being resilient. It deals with overcoming adversities and recovering from setbacks. Adversities and setbacks are a normal part of life. They can be external, such as a sudden pandemic which affects your business negatively. Or adversities can happen internally, such as when conflicts arise about a new direction management wants to take.

In these situations, a leader must be resilient herself, but also help others to be resilient.

Research shows that resilience is fueled by staying positive in the face of obstacles. Unlike the previous six emotions, positivity consists of multiple emotions, such as joy, awe, gratitude, serenity, interest and hope, to name a few. A negative emotional reaction to a setback is normal; however, spiraling into negativity will drain everybody's energy. When expressed or felt too frequently, negativity becomes toxic. Cultivating positive emotions in oneself will make the leader more resilient, and cultivating them in the team or organization will make others more resilient too.

Chapter 7 will explore positive emotions and how to cultivate them.

Summary

Note that the seven leadership behaviors and their emotions that make up the ASPIRE Leadership Model are built from the bottom up. The first three leadership behaviors and their emotional drivers—empathy and caring, compassion and serving and interest and understanding–are focused on meeting the needs of the stakeholders.

The second three leadership behaviors and their emotional drivers–optimism and visioning, inspiration and mobilizing and trust and collaborating–all deal with the need to make change happen. They are action-oriented. The seventh competency, being resilient, deals with overcoming obstacles and staying positive, which is what supports resilience.

Before exploring the seven essential emotions for leading positive, aspirational change in more detail, let me briefly explain why I'm focusing on these seven particular emotions.

A New, Simplified Language of Emotions

In their book, *The Unopened Gift, A Primer in Emotional Literacy*, Dan Newby and Lucy Nuñez describe more than 250 different emotions, and researchers are still discovering new ones. Since such a large number exists, together with the fact that a person can experience a mixture of emotions at any given time, learning about emotions can seem overwhelming. You may not even know where to begin.

That's why I am focusing on the seven most essential emotions for leading change. It's similar to learning a new language. When you begin, your teacher will initially focus on the most important words and sentence constructs that will help you communicate with another person. Learning this new language of emotions in an easy and accessible way will, if practiced, make you a more effective leader and create a positive change in all parts of your life.

I have practiced and taught the seven essential emotions for leading change for many years, but as with learning a language, I benefit from continuing the learning throughout my life. I deeply appreciate the profound change I have seen these suggested incremental steps create for myself and others in our effectiveness to lead the change people aspire to in our professional, public and personal lives.

Who Is This For?

The ASPIRE Leadership Model is for anyone who aspires to create positive, aspirational change. This includes:

- **Formal leaders:** people who are in an organization and in a formal leadership role, such as project, program, team, department and organizational leaders, from first-line manager all the way to C-level and board-level executives.

- **Informal leaders:** people without an official leadership title but who want to create change and therefore must learn to influence without formal power. In organizations, these are the intrapreneurs. In society, these are the community organizers and activists.

- **Entrepreneurs:** people who are undertaking the risk of starting a new business venture.

- **Elected leaders:** people at all levels of society who are elected or aspire to be elected to serve.

- **Those who develop leaders:** executive coaches, leadership development professionals and people managers.

- **Anyone who wants to create positive, aspirational change** for self and by expanding his or her circle of influence for others.

On Your Way to Leading Change

The idea for this book came on the heels of my previous book, *The Boomerang Approach,* which was written to help readers find a role that is aligned with their passions, strengths and needs in the world they care most about. What my readers and coaching clients asked next was, "Now that I'm in my new role, what are the most essential leadership competencies to create the change I aspire to, and how can I learn them without spending too much time?" This book is an answer to that question.

However, to embark on the learning journey to the seven essential emotions for leading change, you don't have to read *The Boomerang Approach*. By discovering and practicing these emotions in Chapters 1–7, you are on your way to developing the leadership behaviors you need to create change.

I recommend that you read the next seven chapters in sequence because the competencies covered in each chapter build on each other. Let me point out that learning these emotions and behaviors is not an all-or-nothing approach. I have already seen great improvements in leaders' effectiveness after they began to practice only one or a few of these new competencies. At the end of each chapter, you have the opportunity to self-assess your level of competence. This will allow you to determine where you may have the greatest need or opportunity for development. Each chapter offers best practices to help you with that development.

Now that you have been introduced to the ASPIRE Leadership Model, let's get started learning more about each of the competencies represented in the model and how you can develop them.

"Not the ones speaking the same language,
but the ones sharing the same feeling understand each other."
~Rumi

CHAPTER 1:
Empathy – The Gate to Caring

Leaders Must Care

Jennifer (name changed) had been an executive in a global telecom company for six months when she hired me for coaching. In our first meeting, she sounded anxious as she explained that her team was not performing well. She was under a great deal of pressure to turn the situation around quickly, or her job would be in jeopardy.

When I asked what she thought the reasons for the performance issues were, she complained that the people on her team weren't putting enough effort into their work. I probed for reasons for their lack of engagement, and she declared, "They are all lazy!"

Following up on this harsh assessment, I learned that during the first six months, she had focused on results without showing any interest or concern for the needs of the people she depended on to produce those results. She'd made little effort to get to know them at a human level. Jennifer's belief was that because they were paid, they should be motivated to give their best. I have observed that to be able to do this, however, they require being treated as human beings with needs, values and emotions. Because Jennifer had regarded her team as a means to an end, they hadn't put in the extra effort to create the turnaround she was hired to produce.

The leader who doesn't appear to care about the people she is leading is not trusted by them, and if a leader is not trusted, people don't follow her.

That is why it is not a surprise that caring organizations have greater engagement of their employees, perform better than their competitors and attract more talent than those that don't have a caring culture. In a caring culture, people show a genuine concern for and interest in the well-being of others, and leaders play an essential role modeling those behaviors. By not caring about her employees, Jennifer had sabotaged her chances for success.

Telling Jennifer that her team's lack of engagement was a result of her not caring about them could make her even more resentful toward them, creating an even greater barrier to caring. Rational arguments about the importance of caring, I've found, are not the best way to develop caring. It requires a deeper emotional shift.

The way to create the kind of shift that opens the gate to caring was first shown to me in an experience I had many years ago.

Emotion That Drives Caring

On a business trip in Asia, I woke up jet-lagged in the middle of the night and turned on the TV to a news story about an ethnic war in Africa. Paramilitary troops of one group were raging through the villages of the other group and mutilating every little child they could find while their fathers, gun pointed at their heads, were forced to watch in horror.

At that moment, thinking of my son at home, I instantly identified with these fathers, and my eyes filled with tears. I imagined myself in their shoes and felt horror, helplessness, deep sadness and anger. I cannot claim that I felt exactly what they were feeling, but I experienced an emotional resonance with their feelings, an emotional empathy.

This opened the gate for my caring about them, but it also created a greater feeling of connectedness with all people, whether they were part of my circle or not. The experience changed my life profoundly in a number of ways, but two insights stood out about how we can learn to care about others who we may not have cared about yet.

The first is that a leader, like any human being of mature age in healthy circumstances, already has the ability to care about others. The difference in our capacity for this relates to who it is that we care about. Naturally, our ability to care about others is stronger for those we are close to or who we identify with. Most mothers' care is focused on the needs of their newborn, and they will prioritize those over the needs of others, including their own. If they didn't, their baby could not survive. We also observe other examples of closeness in relationships that promote caring between children and parents, lovers, spouses, siblings, close friends, colleagues and people of the same group or community. Without our care about the people who are close to us, children would not grow into healthy adults, families would break apart, friendships would not last, and communities and societies could not thrive.

Caring is what makes us human. Who a person cares about in relation to others at a given time can be illustrated by a model of concentric circles of care, each circle representing a person or group of people. Starting with the circle at the center for the person one cares most about, we can then add the next circle representing the next person or group we care about and so on. In that way, we show our relative level of care increasing from the outside in or decreasing from the inside out.

The example below shows four circles, starting with self at the center, then adding the second circle with the people we care about next, such as family and close friends. The third circle represents others in our group such as colleagues or people in our community. The fourth circle, which is labeled "not my group," represents people who we may not be close to or who don't seem like us. Because they are not part of our group, we may care less about them or, in some cases, even feel that they are a threat to us. That's the case when someone objects to giving refugees asylum or, in Jennifer's example, where she labeled her team members "lazy," putting them in a group of people different from how she sees herself.

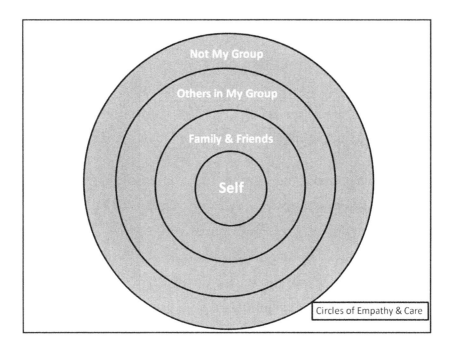

The second insight is that caring about someone can be prompted through the sort of emotional empathy I described earlier, which is the ability to be in resonance with another person's feelings. Note that emotional empathy is different from other types of empathy, such as knowing or understanding what another person thinks, needs or feels. For example, you can understand the sadness of someone else without feeling the person's sadness, or you can understand what the person needs without feeling what the person is feeling when that need is not met, or you can know what the other person thinks. All three are part of what is called cognitive empathy, whereas with emotional empathy, you feel the other person's sadness, including the physical reactions associated with that emotion. You may not feel the exact same emotion, but you are in resonance with the other person's emotion, meaning, for example, you have an emotional reaction to the person's sadness.

Simply recognizing or knowing how another person feels, what they need or how they think may prompt you to care as a learned response, but it does not necessarily lead to caring. However, if you are in resonance with the emotions of someone else, provided that the person is not a psychopath, it prompts an experience of caring about the other, such as I did about those fathers in Africa. Emotional empathy made me feel like I was one of them. Beyond prompting me to care about them, this also created an urge to act on what I felt about their emotional suffering.

An example of the power of emotional empathy as a catalyst for caring at a global scale was the spontaneous expression of care from millions of people around the world after the 9/11 attacks. In Berlin, 200,000 people gathered in the streets with lighted candles. In Moscow, women were sobbing in front of a makeshift tribute on a sidewalk, while in a Kenyan village, Massai people gave their most valuable possession—cows—in a show of support after the attacks.

What does this mean about a leader's ability to learn caring for her stakeholders across distances and differences? An eye-opening example for me was Germany's Chancellor Angela Merkel's response to the 2015 European refugee crisis. At the peak of the crisis in a TV town hall meeting, Merkel very rationally explained why Germany could not possibly accept every single refugee into the country. She had barely finished her argument when a young girl from Syria in the audience started sobbing. As the chancellor listened, the girl shared how much fear and anxiety she and her family were experiencing every day about the possibility of being sent back to her war-torn country. Merkel, visibly moved, spontaneously walked over to comfort the girl. The chancellor, who at one moment had been arguing for restrictive immigration policies in an emotionally detached way, visibly showed emotional empathy for the girl. After that, as the refugee crisis continued to escalate, Merkel, despite strong opposition, made the surprising decision to welcome more than a million refugees into the country.

This shows that a leader can expand her circle of care through emotional empathy. I suggest that this is true for a team leader like Jennifer, the CEO of a large company, as well as for any other leader. No matter where a person is in the hierarchy of an organization or in society, emotional empathy provides a gateway to caring.

While emotional empathy is the most fundamental emotional competence of a leader, becoming absorbed by that feeling for too long carries the risk of burnout, as may happen to a health care professional who experiences the suffering of patients for extended periods of time. I suggest that leaders avoid being absorbed by the feelings related to the suffering of others and instead experience it for a shorter interval, just long enough to prompt caring. Of course, that is easier said than done.

To maintain my capacity for helping others in my work as a leadership coach, I have to empathize with the struggle of another person without getting totally absorbed by their emotions.

Caring and its driver, emotional empathy, are so fundamental to leadership that they build the first layer—foundation—for the other leadership competencies explored in the following six chapters. Just as the foundation of a house needs to be enduringly strong, a leader must have empathy and caring as a strong foundation for all other leadership competencies of the ASPIRE Leadership Model, as illustrated in the three-dimensional pyramid below.

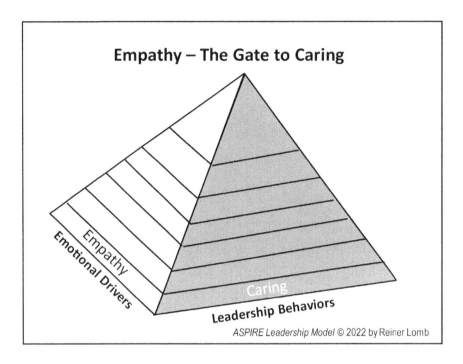

Empathy – The Gate to Caring

Empathy

Emotional Drivers

Caring

Leadership Behaviors

ASPIRE Leadership Model © 2022 by Reiner Lomb

Why is caring, especially about others who are not close to us or are different from us, so hard? Research confirms a lack of empathy, especially emotional empathy, toward people who we don't feel close to or who we perceive as different from us. The good news is that emotional empathy can be learned. But before discussing the ways one can develop it, let's look at the barriers to emotional empathy that need to be overcome to learn it.

Barriers to Empathy and Caring

As described in the previous chapter, shifting to a desired emotional state such as empathy requires a person to first become aware of the emotional state we are in and recognize if it is a barrier to our desired emotional state. With this awareness, we are able to devise strategies that may help us overcome the barriers and make the desired emotional shift. A useful model that helps create awareness about our emotions in regard to our barriers to empathy and care includes three types of emotional regulation systems, each of which are described below. These are the threat, drive and soothing systems.

The threat system alerts us to threats and motivates us to take action. It aims at keeping us alive by constantly scanning for threats in our environment and mobilizing a response to ensure our survival. In times past it helped us to keep safe from or fight a predator. In modern times, it motivates us to act on an approaching deadline. Threat-based emotions include fear, anxiety, anger, jealousy and disgust.

Threat-based emotions are barriers to empathy and care because when these emotional states arise in us in relation to others, we consciously or subconsciously perceive the other person or group as a threat to us and to our safety. Jennifer's perception of her team as lazy led her to regard them as a threat to her meeting her goals. Perceiving them as a threat prompted threat-based emotions such as contempt about their perceived laziness and fear and anger because she viewed them as a threat to her success and, even more basically, to her job security. These threat-based emotions created a barrier to empathy and care.

The drive system is a motivational system that drives you to achieve or acquire the things you need or want. It motivates you to meet your basic needs such as food or shelter as well as your quest for money or such aspirational achievements as career success or social status. Emotions linked to achievement and acquiring important resources include interest and excitement. Your drive system alerts you to opportunities for pursuing your goals and helps you to stay focused in pursuing them. While the drive system is important to achieve and acquire things you need and want, you must be careful that it doesn't get out of balance. Too much focus on achievement and acquiring resources can undermine your interest in the needs of others, as it did for Jennifer. That is why it may not be a surprise that climbing up in the hierarchy often interferes with peoples' ability to have empathy, as research has shown.

People often operate and oscillate mainly between the drive and threat systems and ignore the soothing system, which is the regulation system most vital for keeping an emotional balance in life.

The soothing system, unlike the threat and drive systems that activate you, is associated with the emotional states of feeling safe, calm, content and peaceful. It allows you to soothe yourself and others and is linked with experiences of giving and receiving care, acceptance, encouragement and support. These behaviors can balance the possible toxic effects of the drive and threat systems.

Feeling connected to self and others is linked to your soothing system. Becoming aware of how interconnected you are with others awakens your natural ability to emphasize with and care about people. Feeling disconnected from others, on the other hand, supports a feeling of indifference, which is a barrier to empathy and caring. We can often observe that people feel a strong connection and loyalty to their own group and feel judgmental toward someone who is not part of their group. If this loyalty is not balanced with an understanding of a wider interconnectedness beyond one's own group, it promotes an "us versus them" thinking and becomes a barrier to empathy and caring for people who are not part of their group.

Jennifer made the assessment that her employees were lazy, which in her mind put them in the "lazy group," which are not part of her group. She felt contempt and anger toward them, both barriers to empathy. In reality, they were not lazy, but they were demotivated because they felt distrust toward Jennifer. This was caused by her operating in the drive and threat systems. Emotional empathy would have allowed her to feel their distrust. Then she could have asked, "How can I build trust with my team?" We will go deeper into the emotion of trust in Chapter 6.

In summary, distance, disconnection or division from others can become a barrier to emotional empathy and, with that, a barrier to caring. How can you overcome these things that separate you from others? Following is a list of best practices that can help you get beyond those barriers.

Best Practices to Develop Empathy

To overcome the emotional barriers to empathy that arise out of operating too much in your drive system and threat system—

perceiving someone as a competitor or threat—you must engage your soothing system. You can do this through practices that connect you to yourself and to others.

Connect to Self

Resonating with the emotions someone else is feeling starts with being aware of and in touch with your own emotions and having empathy for yourself. Practicing self-empathy engages your soothing system.

Often, being out of touch with your own emotions, on the other hand, prevents you from creating an emotional resonance with someone else's emotions. Jennifer was not in touch with her own emotions that drove her negative perceptions of her team and her demotivating behaviors toward them. Becoming aware of, getting in touch with and shifting out of her own threat- and drive-based emotions activated Jennifer's soothing system. She became emotionally more balanced, and that opened the door for connecting with her team.

As I coached Jennifer, I emphasized that the first step in this process is to recognize that her behaviors are not working and commit to changing them. The second step is to identify her desired behaviors, such as Jennifer's desire to connect with her team members. The third step is to become aware of what stands in the way of practicing that new behavior, such as the drive- and threat-based emotions Jennifer felt. It was also important to identify the emotions that would support her desired behavior, such as interest in and empathy with the other person. This required her to learn self-awareness through regular practice so that it became an automatic process in her soothing system.

Self-awareness practices focus your attention on your body, your breathing and the thoughts or stories that run through your mind, such as, "I am in danger." These also help you recognize the emotions you are feeling. One way to enter a self-awareness practice is to focus your attention on your breathing for a few minutes. Or you can redirect and focus on other parts of your body or observe your thoughts and emotions without trying to change anything. The goal in those practices is to create awareness, not resolve anything. This will help activate your soothing system so that you are ready to connect to others.

Connect to Others

Often people find it more challenging to empathize with someone they perceive as "not being part of my group" as illustrated earlier by the concentric circles model. The farther out from the center a group appears, the harder it is to connect to that group. It can be compared with the distance of a planet to our earth. The farther away another planet is, the harder it is to reach.

For Ralf (name changed), the "planet" that seemed to be out of reach was a Black immigrant from Africa sitting next to him in a doctor's waiting room in Germany. When I spoke with Ralf, he described his reaction to the man this way: "He looks different from us." Seeing the man aroused Ralf's threat system because he was afraid that immigrants, like the man next to him, would change the culture of Germany. Ralf was afraid that he would become a stranger in his own country. Although he is an outgoing and friendly person, the anxiety Ralf felt in the presence of the African man became a barrier to connect and therefore a barrier to empathize with the man.

Differences that create distance for people and make it hard to connect to others may include a different ethnicity or race, as Ralf experienced it, but it may also be religion, sexual orientation, education, economic or social status or even a different professional role, function or department. In Jennifer's case, the difference between her role as the manager and her team made it hard for her to connect.

Following are two scenarios that show how to connect to others who are not part of your group as a path to develop empathy and care. In the first example, the differences are externally visible, while in the second, the differences are more hidden and may show up only in a conflict situation. Both examples show practical ways to connect with others despite those differences.

Connecting to Others Who Are "Not Part of My Group"

Many years ago, when I was hired for the first time by the Ute Mountain Ute Tribe, a Native American tribe, in Colorado, I had worked with clients from dozens of cultures and countries, but I had no experience in working with indigenous communities. Not knowing what to expect, my drive- and threat-based emotional regulation systems kicked in. On one hand, I was excited about the new challenge and wanted to be as helpful as possible. Yet I was also anxious, not knowing the challenges or the culture of the tribe. So in our first meeting, I asked Chairman Heart, the chairman of the tribe, "What do I need to know so I can best help you?"

His answer was open and direct. In the context of consultants he had worked with, he told me: "Many white people have tried to help us and failed!" This was not an answer that helped calm my anxiety. But rather than allowing my emotional threat system to drive a defensive response, I asked him, "What do you recommend I need to do differently than others who have failed to help you?"

He didn't have to think long and replied, "Before you can help us, first, you have to walk in our moccasins!" Before I could help him, I needed to understand the needs of his tribe, and for him to trust me, he needed to see that I cared. I then asked him, "How would you suggest I do that?" He replied, "Come and visit us on the reservation and talk to our people." Walking in their moccasins, as the chairman called it in his tradition, was a metaphor for practicing empathy.

I took him up on his offer, and our initial conversation led to several visits to their community, where I learned firsthand and through human-to-human connections from the tribal members about their life, their joys and their struggles. It was both joyful and emotionally challenging because of the suffering I was confronted with, such as the high rate of suicide among young people or the rate of poverty that is far exceeding any other ethnic group in the United States. These human-to-human connections helped me understand their needs and thoughts, and it made me resonate with such emotions as pride about their culture, grief about their losses or anxiety about the future of their children. Looking into people's eyes and hearing their voices made me resonate with their suffering and their hopes as if they were my own. I then felt an emotional empathy that made me truly care about the tribe and its future.

Sure, I had read about the tribe's needs and struggle before I arrived at the reservation, and that gave me cognitive empathy, but not emotional empathy. Learning about the tribe through reading created understanding, but meeting people in person, listening to them and spending time in their community created the shift from cognitive to emotional empathy.

For some people, it's exciting to connect to others from a different culture, ethnicity, religion, skin color, sexual orientation, etc., and for others, like Ralf, it may be frightening. In a multi-cultural and highly connected world, the tangible barrier to connect to people outside our bubble or circle has been lowered, but the emotional barriers such as anxiety or fear still exist. Finding the courage to connect with someone "not part of our group" helps to develop empathy and caring.

While in the previous example the barriers to empathy are rooted in the fear of an obvious unknown, in the following example, the differences are more hidden.

Connecting to Bridge Conflicting Values

Gary, the hard-driving sales manager of a midsized manufacturing company, is trying to convince Samantha, head of manufacturing, into a commitment of manufacturing a million units of a new product by the end of next month. To pressure her to agree, Gary tells Samantha, "We will only win this deal if I can go back to the client with this commitment."

But Samantha, whose performance is measured by product quality and meeting her unit commitment (versus Gary, who is measured on revenue) says, "Gary, that is impossible! Producing that many units so quickly won't leave enough time for quality control. I will not commit to that."

Gary, operating in full drive mode, now feels threatened that he is going to lose this big deal. He shifts into the threat system, bursts out in anger and says something offensive to Samantha.

Samantha now feels attacked and shifts into the threat system. She is not only trying to protect the company from making a commitment she thinks it can't fulfill—or could even be sued for—but also protect her own reputation in her professional role. Both leave the call feeling resentment toward the other, which blocks any kind of creative and collaborative conversation they might have to find a solution.

Now imagine an alternative conversation in which Gary and Samantha are making an effort to become aware of the conflicting values their roles hold. They achieve that by postponing judgment, assuming positive intentions of the other person and trying to put themselves in the other person's shoes. By doing that, Gary is now able to ask in a calm tone, "Samantha, what keeps you from making that commitment?" Samantha explains that she is afraid that she wouldn't be able to fulfill the commitment, and the subsequent damage for their company would be costly, and it may even cost her job. Gary responds, "I can understand your hesitation now. What can I do to help you?" Samantha responds, "I understand how important that deal is for you and would like us to win it too. What other options do you think we have to still win the deal?"

Now they have shifted from operating in the drive and threat system to the soothing system. Mutual empathy allows them to understand what is in the way of making the deal happen and allows them to jointly come up with ideas on how to overcome these barriers. As the conversation continues, they come to an agreement to meet jointly with the customer to understand the real customer needs behind this request and discuss alternative delivery options.

In the meeting the customer appreciates the manufacturer's commitment to quality and offers some flexibility about the delivery schedule. Gary and Samantha, by collaborating, are able to work out a schedule that allows them to win the deal without jeopardizing quality.

In this scenario, Gary and Samantha value the differences in their roles and associated values. Through empathy and caring, they bridge their value conflict and create a synergistic partnership that has the potential to create many wins for the company and meet the needs of its clients.

Now let's summarize the key insights from this chapter, and then take a moment to pause and reflect about your own level of emotional empathy.

Summary

- ✓ To be a leader, you must care.

- ✓ Emotional empathy—being in resonance with someone else's emotions—opens the gate to caring.

- ✓ Emotional empathy requires that you connect to your own emotions first—self-empathy. Self-awareness practices help to develop self-empathy.

- ✓ Connecting at a human-to-human level creates emotional empathy.

- ✓ Operating too much in your emotional drive and threat systems (e.g., fear, anxiety, anger, greed, jealousy) is a barrier to empathy.

- ✓ Activating your emotional soothing system by connecting to self and others helps you to overcome these barriers to empathy.

✓ Postponing judgment, assuming positive intentions and trying to put yourself in the other person's shoes will help you connect with others.

Pause and Reflect

Before you begin reading the next chapter, I recommend that you pause a moment and reflect. Think of someone who you feel most challenged by and have a hard time with when it comes to bridging differences. It may be someone in your family, among your friends, at work or within or outside your community or group of people. Visualize that person and ask yourself: "Where am I in my ability to emotionally empathize with that person?"

Use the scale from one to 10, one being the lowest and 10 being the highest to rate emotional empathy for that person.

Emotional empathy: the ability to resonate emotionally with someone else's feelings.

1…2…3…4…5…6…7…8…9…10

If you rate your empathy at seven or lower, ask yourself:

- What is my barrier to emotional empathy for that person? (See barriers above.)

- How could I overcome my barrier? (See practice above.)

- How would that change my behavior or actions toward that person?

Now that we have addressed the importance of caring and how a leader can learn to care through emotional empathy, the next chapter will explore the importance of serving and how the emotion of compassion helps a leader commit to serving.

"The great leader is seen as servant first, and that simple fact
is the key to his greatness."
~Robert K. Greenleaf

CHAPTER 2:
Compassion – The Commitment to Serving

Great Leaders Are Committed to Serve

Great leaders are committed to serve. One of my most memorable leaders was Ann, a lifelong public servant who served three terms as the mayor of Fort Collins, a fast-growing city in Colorado, and was my mentor.

We first met in Germany at an international conference on globalization where Ann and I had been invited to speak. As mayor of Fort Collins, she was representing her city to which I had moved from Germany a few years earlier. As I left the stage after my speech, Ann walked up and introduced herself, adding, "I had no idea that someone like you lived in my city." When I asked what she meant, she told me, "I listened to your speech, and I recognized that you have a lot to offer. Our city needs people like you to engage."

While I gave some thought to what she'd said about engaging with my community, I became curious but anxious at the same time. The many commitments I had with work, travel and family made it difficult to envision or consider adding anything more to my schedule.

During the week, Ann and I were invited to several official events hosted by the two universities who had organized the conference. That gave us the opportunity to spend more time together and for me to introduce my home country to her and to learn about her challenges and hopes for the city she served as mayor. Fort Collins had been on a rapid growth path, and the challenges that came with it included water shortages, air pollution from increased traffic and increased energy needs. I paid specific attention to the issues that were also global issues, such as environmental degradation and climate change, which I had been concerned about for a long time.

Emotion That Commits to Serving

My experience shows that empathizing with and caring about someone's needs does not automatically commit a person to serving those needs. I can sit all day and care about an issue or someone and still not commit to act. I discovered that a commitment to serving the needs of others required more than caring.

After our week together in Germany, Ann and I continued to meet after we got home, and over the course of the next year, she became my mentor. In our meetings I learned as much as I could about the needs and challenges of the city and the leaders who were trying to shape its future. In that process, I was able to meet with other local citizens and eventually join a group that had recently formed to focus on creating a sustainable city. The goal was a city that, in spite of its predicted growth, would be socially, environmentally and economically sustainable for future generations. I joined the steering committee, and we engaged with the key stakeholders, the leaders in the city, to develop a plan and take action. It became some of the most satisfying work I have ever done because, among other things, greenhouse gas emissions in the city were measurably reduced over the coming years.

When Ann first approached me about the possibility of being involved in this service to my community, I was very hesitant because of the demands and needs of my own life. However, as Ann accompanied me as I got to know our community better, I could feel myself caring more and more about its future. I began to develop compassion, which is associated with a commitment to act on my caring.

What I discovered in this process is that to lead change, empathy and caring are prerequisites but are not enough for someone to act on caring. Acting on caring requires a shift to compassion, which is the emotion that is associated with a commitment to serving others in need. I have observed that people often use empathy and compassion interchangeably in everyday conversations. For the purpose of clarity, I want to emphasize that compassion builds on and includes empathy. The previous chapter defined two types of empathy. Cognitive empathy is the intellectual understanding of others' feelings and needs. Emotional empathy is actually feeling the emotions of others as they relate to their suffering or needs.

With that in mind, I offer the following definition of compassion.

Compassion is empathy for the needs and suffering of others and a deep commitment to help alleviate that suffering, meet their needs and ultimately to help promote happiness and fulfillment for them.

With that, compassion builds on empathy, but it also commits a person to act on it. Compassion is usually assumed to be directed toward others, but I emphasize the importance of self-compassion as a gate to compassion. I will share more about that in the section about barriers to compassion below.

Ann was a leader who exemplified this definition of compassion. In the nearly 12 years I knew her, I saw many examples of how Ann's empathy made her care and her compassion committed to serve the needs of the community. Her circle of empathy and compassion reached wide and included those who may have disagreed with her political views. This became visible to me after she died when I attended the memorial service. To my surprise, even leaders which I perceived as her political opponents honored her for her wise counseling with what I felt was sincere appreciation. Their words of gratitude revealed that her circle of compassion included them. They, too, had, through her example, shifted to compassion for their opponent, following in the footsteps of a great servant leader.

As with the circle of empathy and care in Chapter 1, you can use concentric circles to represent who it is that you feel compassion for and whose needs you are motivated and committed to serve. Your circle of compassion may or may not align with your circle of empathy and care because you may have people or groups you care about but aren't ready to commit to serving. Before I met Ann, I was committed to serving the needs of my family, but despite caring about the city we lived in, I was not yet committed to serving its needs. That changed when I expanded my circle of compassion to include the community of people in my new city. As a leader, in order to commit to serving such stakeholders as your employees or clients, you need to extend your circle of compassion to include them.

I must emphasize that to expand your circle of influence as a leader, you have to expand your circle of compassion first, because people won't follow your leadership if they aren't convinced that you care about their needs and are committed to serve them. People recognize if you are a compassionate leader based on the interest you take in their needs and your actions in regard to those needs.

The behavioral leadership competence of serving and its emotional driver, compassion, build the next layer on top of caring and its emotional driver of empathy. Together, these competencies establish the foundation of the ASPIRE Leadership Model for the other five core leadership competencies, as illustrated in the image below.

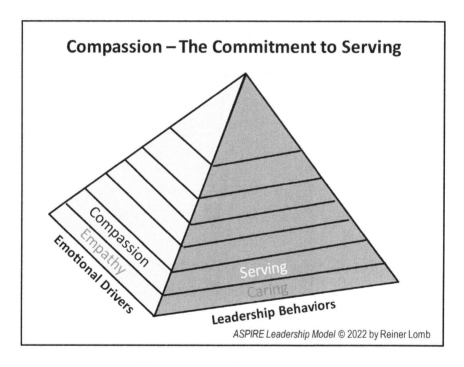

ASPIRE Leadership Model © 2022 by Reiner Lomb

The pyramid illustrates that compassion builds on empathy as explained earlier. This is why I suggest developing empathy first on your way to developing compassion. However, even if you have developed empathy and you care about the needs of a person there may still be barriers that prevent you from committing to act on it, as my own example shows. While I cared deeply about the sustainability of communities and cities, it wasn't until I met Ann that I made the shift to commit to serving.

Barriers to Compassion

Biologist Robert Wright suggests that compassion is not only driven by moral reason but is also built into our gene pool. It is what motivated the behavior that ensured the survival and propagation of our genes by nurturing our offspring, and it helped us to survive and flourish by fostering reciprocal altruism. This means that compassion is an essential driver of behaviors that have helped us survive, evolve and thrive together.

However, our inherent capacity for compassion competes with our inherently selfish and survival-focused behaviors, such as feeding, fighting, fleeing and reproduction. For example, struggling for your own life or that of your offspring may take all your energy and not leave any for others. Therefore, forgive yourself when you struggle to be compassionate on a daily basis because there may be a biological reason why you're not. The good news is that compassion, like empathy, can be learned, as research shows.

Shifting to a desired emotional state such as compassion requires you to first become aware of the emotional state you are in—one that might be a barrier that keeps you from making the shift. Becoming aware of your barriers allows you to better devise strategies to overcome them and make the shift.

Compassion builds on and includes empathy, therefore any barrier to empathy is also a barrier to compassion. As described in Chapter 1, those are the threat-based emotions, such as fear, anxiety, anger, jealousy and disgust, the drive-based emotions, such as interest in and excitement about your desired resources and achievements and, last but not least, the feeling of disconnectedness and distance from others that keeps your soothing system from balancing out your threat- and drive-based emotions.

As with your circles of empathy, the circles of compassion model is useful for creating awareness about who you feel and don't feel compassion for. We often find it is easier to feel compassion for someone we feel close or connected to. These are the people or group of people closer to the center, such as family, friends or community. It can be harder to feel compassion for someone we don't feel connected to or don't consider part of our group. These are represented by the circles farther away from the center.

The question is if you have been able to shift to empathy for the person you struggle to feel compassion for, what else is in the way of shifting to compassion?

Here's an illustration of how this works:

Imagine you are hiking along a raging river. The foaming water makes you feel awe and respect for the power of nature. Suddenly, you hear screaming, and as you rush around the next bend, you see a mother frantically waving her arms and shouting, "Help!

Please help my child!" You see her pointing to a spot in the water where a child is struggling to stay afloat. You feel the fear and panic of the mother and the child. This means you feel emotional empathy, and that makes you care. You would like to help, but the awe and respect for the power of the river have turned into fear for your own life. For only a moment, which feels like eternity, you are undecided. This is the moment where shifting from emotional empathy and care to compassion means that a deep motivation and commitment to act on your caring is required to make the decision to plunge into the raging river and try to save the child.

Shifting from emotional empathy to compassion means you not only feel the distress and understand the need to help but are also committing to do what is required to save the child. Yet the definition of compassion I am using extends beyond the alleviating of suffering and includes empathy for a person's needs beyond the immediate suffering and the commitment to serve those needs. This means that you not only commit to pull the child out of the water but also to help with whatever other needs mother and child may still have afterward, such as medical care or emotional support.

The example shows how challenging it can be to shift from empathy to compassion. Let's look at some of the common barriers that may keep us from making that shift.

Fear

Because it signals danger, fear is a common barrier to compassion, even if a person cares. In the previous example, fear alerts someone to the danger of the river, and it may keep the person from risking his own life. Fear can make him freeze and do nothing, flee or fight. Fighting may mean that he musters up the courage to fight against the forces of the water to rescue the child, such as swimming after the child or using a branch or a rope to pull the child from the water. In my earlier example of initially not committing to serve the city I had moved to, fear of overcommitting on top of my busy travel schedule and of jeopardizing my career had been one of the barriers to shifting from empathy and caring to compassion. Reflecting on my fear, I realized that it was caused by both self-interest and conflicting interests. Here is how both can become barriers to compassion.

Self-Interest

Even though I cared about the future of my city, I was afraid that if I committed to serve, it would take energy and focus away from my work. It was partly the self-interest of my own well-being and my ambition of succeeding in my career that were barriers that I had to overcome to commit to serving the city.

Self-interests are motivated by our threat and drive systems, the emotional regulation systems that motivate us to protect ourselves and meet our basic human needs such as food or shelter as well as our quest for money and such aspirational achievements as career success or social status.

Conflicting Interests

Another barrier that made me hesitate to commit to serve the needs of my new city was two other important interests that conflicted with the possibility of volunteering. One was related to my family, as I believed that committing to serve the wider community would take away from my ability to spend enough time with them. The second was related to the commitment I had made to my manager and colleagues back in Germany. I had relocated to the United States to expand our business globally. I was convinced that in order to help make this effort successful, my full attention was required. I believed that taking on other commitments would jeopardize my ability to fulfill that commitment. In my personal value system, you keep your word. Therefore, I had created a "moral" justification for my hesitation to commit to another cause I deeply cared about, but that justification did not resolve my inner conflict.

Illusion of Separateness

In his novel *The Plague* Albert Camus describes the illusion of separateness. In the story, people are trapped in a city that suffers under the plague. It is sealed off to prevent the spreading of the deadly virus, and nobody is allowed to leave. The protagonist, who has a girlfriend outside the city, is faced with the decision to take advantage of an opportunity to be smuggled out. Leaving means he can live and be happy, although with the risk of spreading the disease. Staying means his possible death. As he is struggling with his decision, he is told that there is "no shame in choosing happiness," and he replies, but "there may be a shame in being happy all by oneself." He realizes that separateness, which means that he could be happy while others suffer, is only an illusion. That sudden awareness makes him decide to stay and join a group that takes care of the vulnerable.

Conflicting Values

One of the conflicts between people, such as those from different cultures, different groups within a society or even within organizations, is a conflict in values. In my work around the world, I have observed that such differences can affect a person's ability to feel compassion for a person from the other group.

Let's take the example of Max, who comes from a country where being on time is very important, and he has scheduled his first meeting with Fernando, who comes from a country in which arriving at a meeting late is acceptable. Fernando arrives 15 minutes late, not realizing that this would be an issue for Max, so Fernando doesn't apologize. Yet Max, before he even has a chance to get to know Fernando, has already judged him as unreliable and disrespectful. Then, later in the meeting, Fernando asks Max for help with something he needs, but Max, in the back of his mind, believes that Fernando doesn't deserve his help because in Max's view Fernando acted disrespectfully. This judgment based on his own values and without awareness of Fernando's different values prevents Max from feeling compassion and committing to help.

Lack of Self-Compassion

In the same way that being judgmental is a barrier to compassion, being self-judgmental is a barrier to self-compassion. Research shows that self-compassionate people are better able to create mutually supportive friendships than those who are self-critical. This means that in some cases, you first need to develop compassion for yourself before you can develop compassion for others, as the following story shared by Kristin Neff in her book *Self-Compassion* shows.

As a young mother she was on an airplane with her 2-year-old autistic son. After the plane took off, the child started crying without any visible cause. When she could not silence him, the other passengers appeared frustrated, turning their heads and giving disapproving looks, or so she perceived. In her feelings of self-judgment because she could not quiet her son, she felt embarrassed and judged as not being a good mother. She then tried to escape with the child to the restroom. But the door was locked. She was forced to wait outside while her son continued crying. Standing there in the open, drawing others' attention, made her feel even more the target of their disapproval.

As she surrendered to this feeling of helplessness, she was surprised when a feeling of self-compassion suddenly came over her. She instantly felt calmer. The situation wasn't her fault, she realized.

She was doing the best she could. As she became calmer, her son stopped crying.

Her feeling of judging herself had been a barrier to feeling compassion for her son. Shifting to self-compassion served as a gateway for that and allowed her to serve his needs. He needed to feel that he was safe with his mother. Her calming presence served that need. After that, she was able to take her child back to their seat and continue the flight peacefully.

Now that you have read about some of the barriers to compassion, I encourage you to pause and reflect. Ask yourself, "Which of these barriers have I experienced?" The following section provides some best practices that may help you overcome those barriers.

Developing Compassion: Best Practices

In my experience, developing compassion becomes more practical when you have a specific person or group of people in mind that you want to develop compassion for. It then starts with identifying who you need or want to develop compassion for, as described in the first exercise, and then, depending on your barriers to compassion for that person or group of people, choosing the right practice(s) from the following list.

Identify Who to Develop Compassion For

Start with thinking of the people or groups of people who are important stakeholders for you, such as your employees or clients. From that list, choose someone who you care about but who you struggle to feel compassion for. Remember, feeling compassion for someone is the emotion associated with having empathy and a deep commitment to serving the needs of that person.

Reflect on the barriers that, despite your care, keep you from feeling compassion for that person or group. This may be one or more of the barriers listed above or a different barrier you can identify. It could be a strongly held belief about that person, such as, "This person doesn't deserve my compassion," or, "Helping this person would be in conflict with my own interest." Or it may be an emotional barrier, such as the fear I felt in my earlier example about overcommitting, or even a fear you may have of that person. In the earlier example about separateness, Camus' protagonist, before committing to take care of the people who had the plague, had to overcome his fear of getting infected himself. If you recognize at any point that you don't care enough about another's well-being, I suggest you start with developing emotional empathy first, as described in Chapter 1.

Identifying your barriers to compassion helps you to identify strategies to overcome them. For example, knowing that lack of self-compassion is a barrier to compassion naturally points you to developing self-compassion. Identifying self-interest as a barrier to compassion points you toward focusing on the practice that may help to transcend self-interest. Following are some best practices.

Developing Self-Compassion

You may have judged yourself as not worthy when things didn't go so well, such as when you failed at something important to you or you felt judged by others, like the young mother who had a hard time calming her child on a flight. She perceived the looks of the other passengers as a judgment that she was a bad mother, and that made her judge herself in the same negative way.

The approach I suggest when you fail at something and are about to blame yourself is to postpone your self-blaming, self-criticizing or self-judgment. Be kind to yourself and be aware of your negative thoughts about yourself, such as, "I am such a failure," or, "I am not good enough." Replace such negative thoughts by telling yourself, "I had good intentions," "I am human, and like other humans, I can fail," and, "I am determined to learn from this."

In our social media world, people often share their successes and happy moments and not their failures or weaknesses. That might give you the false impression that you are the only one failing at something. Failure can make you feel more vulnerable, and putting yourself down does not help you feel better. Instead, use your emotional energy to focus on becoming a better version of yourself without comparing yourself with others.

Deep and profound learning can come from major failures or breakdowns in life. In order to use such breakdowns for personal growth, ask yourself, "What can I learn from this difficult experience that I may not have learned yet?" Sometimes, you may have to stay in that question for a while with patience until a new insight emerges. When that occurs, ask yourself, "How will I apply this new learning?"

If your mind is still cycling through negative thoughts about what has happened to you, accept what has happened as something that is now in the past. You don't have to like what has happened, but you can accept it as something that you cannot change.

Overcoming Fear

This practice is about using fear to shift to compassion instead of being blocked by it. For example, my fear of overcommitting was caused by not knowing what committing to serve in my new city really would mean in terms of time, effort and knowledge. I didn't even know what I didn't know, yet I was assuming that a commitment to serve the city would be in conflict with my commitment to my family and my work.

Through Ann's mentoring, I learned how I could use my passions, competencies and experiences in service to my city without overcommitting and having my family suffer. She helped me see how valuable and unique my experiences were and how I could use them to support the city's environmental efforts. I was passionate about addressing this issue at a local level. I had leadership experience and competencies from my professional life, specifically how to identify and engage with key stakeholders. I also knew how to partner with people who had experiences that complemented mine, and I realized through consultation with Ann that I could do it with less effort and time commitment than I had assumed. So I identified a citizen group whose interest aligned with mine, and I eased my way into attending the group's weekly meetings, where I helped strategize the development of a sustainable community. Suddenly, fear of overcommitting disappeared because I learned that by attending one meeting a week, I could serve and still have enough time for family and work commitments. By becoming aware of the cause of my fear and acquiring a new perspective on how to overcome it, through the help of an experienced mentor, I was able to shift to compassion.

Transcending Self-Interest

Prioritizing self-interest over the needs of others is a barrier to compassion. Experiences that allow an orbital or overview perspective can help transcend self-interest. Leland Melvin, an African American astronaut, describes how he gained such a change in perspective during his first mission to the space station. At one point, he was invited to the Russian segment of the station to share a meal. While breaking bread and viewing the Earth with colleagues from different countries, some of whom had previously fought wars against each other, including Russia, France, Germany and the United States, he suddenly had a cognitive shift that made him see the enormity and interconnectedness of what he called "our blue marble." Here Leland recognized that just as it is on the space station it is in the interest of all people around the world to work together to survive and thrive.

The protagonist in Camus' novel had a similar realization when he became aware that his idea of separateness—that he could be happy while others suffer—was only an illusion. He suddenly realized his interconnectedness with all humans, and it transcended his self-interest. Instead of using his chance to escape the city ravaged by the plague, he decided to stay and help take care of the sick, even at his own risk of getting infected and dying.

This exercise is an invitation to shift to an orbital perspective, like the one Leland Marvin experienced. Imagine sitting at a table with people from around the world and breaking bread and viewing your common home, our planet, together. Become aware that you are breathing the same air, drinking from the same water, feeding your families from the same soil or from the same ocean. Become aware that threats such as those from a nuclear war, pandemics, environmental disasters, climate change or mass migration due to regional conflicts are a common threat to all of humanity.

As Leland shared the meal with Russian, German and French colleagues, he was an African American who represented his country but was denied equal status in that country. He knew the experience of separation, exclusion and injustice. Yet he found the ability to see the real interconnectedness among those gathered there despite his own experience as a Black man. This is the beneficial power of the higher, orbital view. Like Leland Marvin, try to take an orbital view and become aware of our common humanity and feel how you are interconnected and interdependent with others that may not be part of your group.

Overcoming Conflicting Values

If your barrier to developing compassion is based on your belief that the other person doesn't deserve your compassion because the person's behavior is in conflict with your own values, the way to overcome the barrier is to understand the other person's real intentions. In the earlier example of Max and Fernando, for Max, being on time means being there no later than the agreed-upon time, while for Fernando, being 15 minutes late means still being on time. Max falsely assumes bad intentions from Fernando because Max perceives his lateness as a sign of disrespect. Max feels disrespected and angry. His emotional threat system is activated, and it becomes a barrier to feeling compassion for Fernando. Each culture has its own set of values, and conflict of values, like the one described, is a common barrier to compassion.

Examples of a conflict of values between people replay millions and millions of times around the world whenever people from different cultures interact. That includes not only people from different ethnicities and countries but also people in the workplace who hold competing values because of their different roles, such as sales, manufacturing, human resources and so on. Each of these people in their different roles are measured on different outcomes, such as the salesperson who is measured on sales versus the manufacturing person who is measured on producing a product at a committed volume and quality.

The question now is how can we change our belief that the other person doesn't deserve our compassion because of the described values conflict? There are two behaviors I suggest and that many of those I have coached found useful. The first is to postpone judgment about the other person whose behavior you dislike. Postponing judgment will give you time to understand the reason for the other person's behavior before you react and possibly damage the relationship. The second behavior is to assume that the other person has positive intentions. For example, Fernando had no intention to show disrespect toward Max. In fact, the opposite was true.

Both of these behaviors—postponing judgment and assuming positive intentions—give you time and the right emotional state to learn and understand the reasons for the behavior that frustrates you. For example, Max, once he has built a relationship with Fernando, will find out that in Fernando's culture being 15 minutes late is accepted and not meant to show disrespect. Then they can talk openly about how to bridge that value conflict in regard to time in the future.

Now, let's summarize the key insights from this chapter, and then take a moment to pause and reflect about your own level of compassion.

Summary

- ✓ A leader must be committed to serve.

- ✓ After caring, it is the second of the seven essential leadership behaviors for creating positive change.

- ✓ While emotional empathy makes a person care about the needs of others, caring by itself does not necessarily lead to action.

- ✓ Serving is the behavior that acts on caring.

- ✓ The emotion that drives a person to serve is compassion.

- ✓ Research shows that compassion can be developed. The question is how?

- ✓ In order to develop compassion:

  - We must understand who we need to develop compassion for.

  - We must know what our barriers are to developing compassion for that person or group of people.

  - We must then choose the right strategy and practice that helps us overcome those barriers and develop compassion.

Pause and Reflect

Before you continue reading, I recommend pausing a moment and choosing a person, such as a colleague, friend, family member, boss, employee, client, etc., who you care about but whose behavior you are most challenged by. Then ask yourself, "On a scale from one to 10, one being the lowest and 10 being the highest, what is my level of compassion for this person?" In other words, how much empathy do you have for the needs of this person, and how strong is your commitment to help meet those needs?

Compassion Test:

1...2...3...4...5...6...7...8...9...10

If your compassion is seven or lower, ask yourself:

- What are my biggest barriers to compassion? See list above as a starting point, or identify barriers that are not on that list.

- What strategy or practice can I use to overcome my barriers? See list of best practices above, or come up with your own.

- How will feeling compassion allow me to behave or act differently toward that person?

- How might that change the person's behavior or actions?

Now that we have addressed the importance of serving for a leader and how a leader can commit to serving through compassion, the next chapter will explore the importance of understanding and how the emotion of interest helps a leader to understand.

"No one can do inspired work without genuine interest in his subject and understanding of its characteristics."
~Andreas Feininger

CHAPTER 3:
Interest – The Key to Understanding

Before Acting, Leaders Must Understand

Trying to understand before you act is important advice for anyone, but it's absolutely critical for you as a leader because of the impact your decisions have on your team, organization or society. Trying to understand a particular problem, person or situation is difficult when you believe you know the answer already or when an unconscious bias makes you take a shortcut to judgment. The following personal example has made me appreciate this even more.

During a break on the last day of a weeklong workshop, Nancy (name changed), one of the participants, asked me, "Could I talk to you in private?" "Sure," I said and we proceeded to a quiet area. She looked troubled as she said, "I want to apologize to you!"

When I asked why, she exclaimed, "For hating you without even knowing you!"

I was puzzled because up until then we hadn't had the opportunity to talk in person. How could she feel such a strong animosity toward me? She explained, "I am Jewish and a grandchild of both Holocaust victims and survivors. I grew up hearing about the horrible crimes committed by the Germans against my family. When I heard your accent, I saw in you the perpetrators who did this to my family."

Tears were running down her face as she shared this. My accent had triggered a replay of the intergenerational trauma from her family's experience during WWII. I could empathize with her because of my own family's trauma from that war. I tried to comfort her by saying, "You don't need to apologize. I understand how you could feel that way toward me. It's not your fault."

Throughout my life, I've had experiences of meeting people who felt animosity toward me when they learned I was from Germany, or upon hearing my German accent, because of the crimes Nazi Germany had committed. In those cases, people didn't want to engage with me and would ignore me or turn away. Or they would confide their feelings about me to others, who then shared with me how the person felt toward me. I knew their emotional reaction had nothing to do with who I was, so I never took it personally but had always wished that the person would have talked directly to me about it.

That's why what Nancy had done was a gift to me. She was the first one who openly shared how she was feeling toward me and the first to apologize about it, and she allowed me to apologize for the crimes my country had committed against her family. She opened the door for the type of conversation I had been interested in for a long time.

What made me relate to Nancy's pain, though I didn't share this with her at the time, was that I had also grown up with a story of loss and pain. My mother's family is mixed German-Czech and was driven from their home in what was known as Czechoslovakia before it dissolved into the independent states of the Czech Republic and Slovakia. One of my mother's brothers went missing in action and was never found. Another brother died as a prisoner of war. My grandmother never fully recovered from those losses and died, still grieving, when I was a child. My experience of witnessing the suffering of my mother and grandparents from early childhood made it easier for me to emotionally resonate with Nancy's experience of the trauma passed on to her.

Interest Is the Key to Understanding

As my interest in Nancy's initial feeling about me as a German was the key to understanding why she felt that way, the emotion of interest in general is the key to understanding. Interest can be described as a state of fascination in which you are pulled to explore and immerse yourself in what you are discovering. In that state, you feel open and alive and feel your horizon expanding and, with it, your possibilities. While interest in a subject is the key for you to understand that subject, interest in another person is the key for you to understand that person. The emotion of interest in others builds on the emotions of empathy and compassion for them, and vice versa.

Despite her initial animosity toward me, Nancy became interested in what I had to say. Throughout the following days, instead of turning away when I talked, she listened when I spoke. Her shift from initially feeling hatred toward me to becoming interested in who I really was allowed her to understand me better. Nancy came to understand that, from the depth of my heart, I condemned the crimes committed by Nazi Germany. She had opened the door for me to say, "I am sorry about what happened to your family." In addition, my empathy with the pain that continues to live on in families of Holocaust victims and survivors inspired in me a lifelong interest—in pursuit of understanding—in the history of the crimes committed by my country.

How can you, like Nancy, expand your circle of interest to include people who you feel challenged by or may even perceive as enemies? In the workplace, this may be the team member, boss or client who gives you trouble or makes you feel anxious. In your community, this may be a difficult neighbor or people from another group you feel threatened by, such as someone from another religion, political party, ethnicity, skin color or societal status.

One example of someone bridging such a divide and expanding his circle of interest is Daryl Davis, an African American blues musician who became an anti-racism activist. Because he is Black, Daryl has experienced hatred directed toward him since childhood. During those encounters, he would often ask himself, "How can they hate me if they don't even know me?" For Daryl, this was not just a rhetorical question. He really wanted to understand at a deeper level why he was hated.

One night in a club where Daryl played music, a man, who later identified himself as a member of the Klu Klux Klan, introduced himself to Daryl because he liked his music. When the man openly shared his racist beliefs, Daryl, instead of turning away or getting angry, stayed engaged in the conversation. He was interested in learning more about the man and his perspective. One of the beliefs the man shared was that all Black people have within them the gene that makes them violent. Daryl, instead of rejecting the claim, asked the man to name three Black serial killers. When the man couldn't come up with any, Daryl easily rattled off a handful of white serial killers, asserting that whites are predisposed to becoming serial killers. The Klansman objected and Daryl admitted that what he'd asserted about whites was false, but no more so than what the man had said to him.

This began a connection and process that led to the Klansman eventually questioning his beliefs. Five months later, he announced to Daryl that he had left the Klan. He had realized through their conversations that his old belief system was not true. Daryl, encouraged by this experience, continued to study the beliefs and structure of the KKK to such a degree that he often understood these even better than many of the Klansmen. In that process, over more than 30 years, Daryl got to know many Klansmen, and through his committed effort to make them question their beliefs, he inspired more than 200 members to leave the Klan. Some even became anti-racism activists.

Daryl's approach in which he listened to understand and respectfully questioned assumptions is a powerful lesson about cultivating interest in others who we feel challenged or even threatened by. At the heart of his approach is a willingness to understand the other person's needs, beliefs and the emotions that drive his behavior as well as the system he lives and operates in.

But to truly understand what drove the man's behavior, Daryl first had to be empathetic. That allowed him to see the man as a human being who has the need to feel safe, and he understood how the man's false beliefs about Black people made him feel threatened in his safety. Through empathy, Daryl understood that this is what fueled the man's fear and ultimately his hatred of Black people. He could speak to that fear and prove that it was based on an unfounded assumption and dissolve it.

Daryl's example underlines the importance of understanding an issue. He says that the best thing one can do is to study up on the subject as much as possible. By showing that he understood the Klan's organization and belief system, including what motivates its hatred toward Blacks, Daryl gained respect and opened the door for conversations with many of the Klansmen. What motivated him to gain that level of understanding was interest, which was triggered by his initial curiosity about why he was hated. It is only from that kind of deeper understanding that a leader can inspire others to change their behaviors. Developing interest in the needs and issues of stakeholders is a critical competency for leaders inside and outside of organizations.

People often use interest and curiosity interchangeably, but there is an important difference some academic researchers make. They suggest that curiosity is the emotion that is driven by the negative feeling of having a knowledge gap, such as the curiosity that made Daryl ask why someone would hate him when they didn't even know him. Once a person has an answer that closes the knowledge gap, the person's curiosity is satisfied and ends the search for more information.

Interest, on the other hand, will motivate you to keep searching for information to understand a subject more fully. Your commitment to the time required and the purpose involved is more sustained. While curiosity is not a sustained driver for gaining understanding, it can be a very strong trigger for an emerging interest, as it was in Daryl's case. It was his curiosity that made him ask why someone would hate him when they didn't even know him. But it was his interest that motivated him to gain a deeper understanding of the Klan's belief system, and it has motivated him to become a lifelong activist against racism.

It is essential that leaders understand those they want to serve and influence. Interest is the key to gaining that understanding, regardless of the leader's role or the type of organization. Developing an understanding of stakeholders' needs, circumstances and what would meet their needs enables leaders to serve and influence stakeholders.

Interest and understanding build on empathy, which motivates a leader to seek out opportunities to put himself into another person's shoes. Leaders also need compassion, which is the deep commitment to serve the needs of others and help them flourish. Last but not least, effective leaders want to truly understand what drives people's behavior so they can influence that behavior positively not to manipulate but to serve their needs. This requires a deep and sustained interest in both the people they serve and the systems or solutions that serve those needs.

Therefore, empathy, which makes a leader care, compassion, which commits a leader to serve, and interest, which motivates a leader to understand, are the emotional competencies that build the foundation of the ASPIRE Leadership Model represented by the pyramid below.

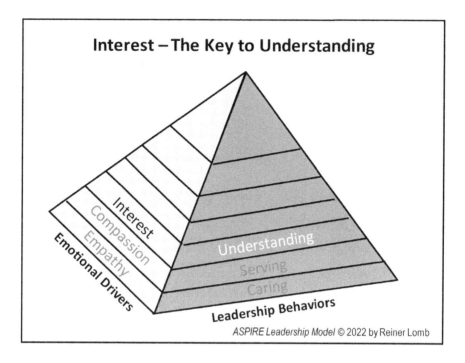

Interest – The Key to Understanding

Interest
Compassion
Empathy
Emotional Drivers

Understanding
Serving
Caring
Leadership Behaviors

ASPIRE Leadership Model © 2022 by Reiner Lomb

While empathy builds the foundation for developing compassion, and empathy and compassion are important emotional drivers of interest in others, interest, in return, can also open the door to empathy and compassion. That's because interest helps us understand, and a better understanding of others can lead to empathy and compassion.

Barriers to Interest

Interest, like empathy and compassion, can be developed. Before going into some best practices for developing it, let's first review some of the barriers to interest.

Emotions are caused by your assessment of what is happening, which may be different than what is actually happening. Some assessments arouse your interest, and others are a barrier to interest. When you perceive information or an experience as new, valuable, unexpected, surprising and comprehensible, it increases your interest. However, if you perceive what you encounter as nothing new, not of value, too difficult to process, incomprehensible or even dangerous, it makes you lose interest.

The following is a list of barriers to interest that I have encountered frequently. It is not meant to be a complete list but rather a starting point for becoming aware of your own barriers to interest. I encourage you to use the questions included in each description of a particular barrier to reflect on your own barriers to interest. The first four are barriers to interest in understanding others. The last four are barriers to interest in understanding an issue or subject.

Lack of Caring

Not caring or feeling indifferent about the needs of another person is a barrier to interest. That's why in the ASPIRE Leadership Model, empathy (caring) and compassion (commitment to serving) are positioned as a foundation for interest. I encourage you to test this by thinking of someone who is on the outside of your circles of empathy and compassion. Envision that person. How interested are you in understanding their needs and possible solutions that could meet their needs? If your answer is very little or not at all, lack of caring may be one of your barriers to interest in regard to this person.

Feeling Fear, Anger or Resentment

Emotions related to your emotional threat system, such as fear, anger or resentment, are barriers to interest. Can you recall a situation where someone's action made you angry or resentful? In this emotional state, how much interest did you feel in trying to understand the other person? If your answer is very little or none, this is a barrier to interest in understanding that person's needs. When your brain is hijacked by fear or anger, you need to calm your mind before you can feel interest in understanding what is really going on.

Feeling Distrust

Think of someone who you distrust. When you engaged with that person, how much interest did you feel in understanding them? If your answer is very little or none, distrust may be one of your barriers. Please note that trust has multiple dimensions, and you will learn about those in Chapter 6.

Believing You Know Better

Remember a challenging or even heated conversation you had with someone. Maybe you thought, "I know better than this person." If so, feelings such as arrogance or righteousness may have been barriers to your interest in understanding that person's perspective or insights. Arrogance is associated with believing strongly in your perspective and not being open to the ones that differ from yours. Righteousness, while similar, is associated with believing that your beliefs are the only correct beliefs. Another emotion associated with looking down on others is contempt, which is associated with your assessment that the person is not aligned with your values. Such a conflict of values may also keep you from being interested in the other's perspective.

Believing You Won't Be Able to Understand

The belief "I won't be able to understand" can keep you from engaging with an issue or subject. Recall a time when you had to understand something new, maybe at school or work. You may have thought, "This is too confusing and complicated. I won't be able to understand." "I am not smart enough to understand this," or, "I am not good at this subject." If you had any of those thoughts, you probably weren't able to connect with the content or didn't feel positively about what you were trying to understand and therefore lost interest.

Believing You Should Already Know

Have you ever thought, "I should already know this," or, "I should have the answer"? Beliefs like this are a barrier to interest because they can lead to the behavior of jumping all too quickly to an answer without taking time to understand the subject. Our traditional educational system and corporate system have rewarded those who have an answer rather than those who are asking the best questions. Jumping to an answer too quickly prevents you from taking time to come up with a better question to ask. The answer is then often the person's opinion, which others might mistake as a fact. This creates a false sense of certainty, especially if it comes from a person of authority. Certainty is associated with believing that you already know everything you need to about something and don't need to learn more about it. It may show up as a tendency to hold on to strong opinions and an unwillingness to question your own beliefs.

Believing There Is Nothing New or of Value Here for You

You may recall a situation in which you felt bored when you were asked to engage in a topic. Feeling bored is associated with the assessment, "There is nothing new or of value here for me." That assessment is a barrier to interest. Interpreting something as "not new" or "not of value" may help you to not waste time in routine situations, but it can become a major barrier to learning something new and important. If "nothing new or of value here" is your assessment when you face a topic, it will prevent you from feeling interested. Feeling bored can be a warning sign. The addiction to newness can be observed in the social media world, where content is constantly being tailored to bite-sized information and labeled "Breaking News" to gain people's attention. The addiction to newness is a barrier to interest and understanding.

You Don't Find Something Enjoyable

You may have tried to study something that you didn't find enjoyable. How did that affect your interest in the subject? Maybe your mind or your attention wandered to something you did enjoy. People tend to withdraw the moment something stops being enjoyable, even if they are expected to stay in the class or meeting. They then disengage. If you don't enjoy a subject or content, your interest easily drops. Disliking the experience of engaging in a specific subject or content is a barrier to interest and understanding.

At this point, I encourage you to pause and take note of your own barriers to interest that you may have identified from the previous list. Which of the emotions do you feel, or what previous stories (assessments) about something run in the back of your mind when you lack or lose interest? Keep these barriers in mind when reading through the following best practices for developing interest, and choose the practices that can best help you overcome your specific barriers to interest.

Developing Interest: Best Practices

Two domains of interest are critical for a leader: interest in understanding the human needs of the leader's key stakeholders and interest in understanding the circumstances, systems or solutions that affect or meet those needs. Aligning the needs of your stakeholders with your own higher aspirations will drive your interest in those stakeholders. It helps you care deeply about your stakeholders' needs.

Daryl Davis recognized the importance of aligning his aspiration to overcome racism with the Klansman's need to overcome a fear of Black people, even if the Klansman was not aware of it. This alignment helped Daryl connect and also created his sustained interest.

Developing interest starts with creating self-awareness about your stakeholders, their needs, including their aspirational needs, and the systems and solutions that serve those needs. This builds on your ability to empathize with others. Chapter 1 explains emotional empathy as a gate to caring, which is the type of empathy that makes you resonate with the emotions of another person. Understanding the needs of others requires another type of empathy, cognitive empathy, which requires you to ask people the right questions and listen.

Your circles of compassion from the previous chapter represent the stakeholders whose needs you want to understand. Starting with yourself at the center and then progressing outward, ask, "How well do I understand the needs of that person or group of people?" If your answer is "not very well," ask yourself, "How interested am I in that person's needs?" If your answer is "very little," reflect on your barriers to interest. Make your best guess about which barriers keep you from feeling interested in the needs of that stakeholder.

For example, is it lack of caring about or lack of commitment to serve the stakeholder? If that's the case, you may want to revisit Chapters 1 and 2 to help develop your ability to care for and commit to serving these people. Caring about and commitment to serving someone drives interest because it motivates you to understand your stakeholders' needs and the best way to meet those needs.

If you understand someone's needs, you can have a better foundation for understanding the solutions that may serve those needs. Daryl Davis first made sure he understood the needs and false beliefs of the KKK. Then he compared the false beliefs with the facts and devised strategies for his conversations, which were his solutions that helped change the Klansman's beliefs. Daryl's interest was his key to gaining understanding.

To sustain his interest, he had to avoid being held back by resentment, fear and anger. That's why understanding and overcoming them is so critical for maintaining interest. Had he allowed himself to be absorbed by the fight-or-flight response of those threat-based emotions, he wouldn't have been able to listen as empathetically and communicate as effectively as he did.

Now let's assume you care about and are committed to serving your stakeholders but are still struggling to feel a sustained interest in understanding their needs and the solutions that meet those needs. Following are best practices that will help you overcome other barriers to interest you might have.

Calming Your Mind

Emotions related to your emotional threat system, such as fear, anger or resentment, are barriers to interest because all your energy is taken by your fight, flight or freeze response. When your brain is hijacked by fear or anger, you first need to calm your mind before you can feel interest in understanding what is going on. The self-awareness practices in Chapter 1 that activate your soothing system, such as focusing your attention on your breathing, your body and your thoughts, without trying to resolve anything help to calm your mind.

Creating a Window of Trust

While distrust is the emotion that can protect you from possible harm caused by another person, it keeps you from engaging with that person and becomes a barrier to interest. It's a double-edged sword that, while it may protect you, it also robs you of the opportunity to gain a better understanding of someone.

If you have an important stakeholder whom you distrust, how can you gain a better understanding about that person while protecting yourself? My suggestion is to create a window of trust big enough to peek through with interest without exposing yourself to too much risk. Daryl practiced this by engaging with the Klansmen with prudence.

Staying calm, as suggested in the previous practice, helped him to engage with full awareness and alertness. Daryl created a small window of trust through which he listened and gained understanding. Chapter 6 will go deeper into the different dimensions of trust.

Being Open to Learning

In our divided world, the perception "I know better than the other person" is quite common, no matter which side of the conversation we're on. I observe it regularly in public discourse, in organizations and even in families. Believing strongly in your opinion and not being open to the ones that differ from yours (arrogance), believing that your beliefs are the only correct beliefs (righteousness) or believing values different from yours are unacceptable (contempt) shut down opportunities for listening and gaining understanding. Being open to understanding another person doesn't mean you have to give up your values or beliefs. It means you are open to learning something new. Entering the conversation with openness helps to overcome the "I know better than the other person" barrier to interest.

Ways of Listening

A belief such as "I won't be able to understand" becomes a barrier to interest because you're not easily able to connect to content you find confusing or complex. Beliefs like these may, for example, keep you from listening to an expert on the subject. Connecting to the content in some way, on the other hand, will help to arouse your interest. In that case, your way of listening is to listen for something that is familiar. The risk of listening that way, however, is that you search for information that confirms what you already know, and once you find that information, you lose interest and aren't learning anything new. Had Daryl listened only for

REINER LOMB • 91

information that confirmed what he already knew, that the Klansman was racist, the conversation would have ended there.

The second way of listening is to listen for new information that possibly challenges what you know already. Daryl did that and learned that the Klansman held the false belief that Black people are genetically predisposed to become violent.

Daryl also used empathic listening, which is tuning into what the other person feels, thinks and needs. This third kind of listening helped Daryl understand that the Klansman's fear of Black people was due to his false belief that they are violent.

A fourth way of listening is generative, which means you listen for new possibilities that might be created in a situation.

For Daryl, this involved listening for the possibility that the initial Klansman he had a conversation with might have a change of heart once his beliefs have changed. Listening not just to confirm what we already know but for something new or disconfirming, combined with empathic listening and generative listening, allows us to connect with the person. This connection is what fuels interest, helps us gain understanding and opens the door to new possibilities.

Say, "I Don't Know"

If you have the tendency to jump too quickly to an answer because you think, "I should already know this," or, "I should have the answer," practice saying, "I don't know." By saying this, you open yourself to learning. Jumping to an answer prevents further interest as well as any possibilities for gaining new understanding. Saying, "I don't know," requires us to feel at peace with not knowing, of course. As a leader, saying, "I don't know. What do you think?" invites others to share and create a culture of co-creating answers. When everybody learns together, the group can create more possibilities for action. Saying, "I don't know," unleashes that potential.

Awe, Wonder, Perplexity and Ambition Support Learning

Feeling bored, confused or joyless when engaging in specific discussion or content can become an emotional barrier to your interest in that subject. The stories associated with those emotions, such as, "There is nothing new or of value," or, "I don't know what's going on here, and I don't like it," take all your energy. This prevents you from engaging in the subject. On the other hand, when you feel perplexity, awe or ambition, it can help you become curious and interested in gaining new understanding and learning. Wonder then builds on perplexity. It is associated with the story "I don't know, but what an excellent opportunity this represents."

Awe is similar to wonder, but it adds the element of profound joy and gratitude about what you are experiencing. Awe is also described as the feeling of being in the presence of something vast that transcends your understanding of the world. Awe might make you feel small and fearful or sometimes might stimulate curiosity and interest in what you don't understand. Ambition is the emotion that is associated with the belief that life has possibilities for you and you are going to realize them.

Shifting into the moods of perplexity, wonder, awe and ambition by practicing the language associated with these will fuel your interest.

What Would Be a Better Question?

The last practice I suggest that helps to fuel interest is to articulate the right question. Daryl changed the question, "Why are you racist?" to "Why do you hate me even when you don't know me?"

The second, stronger question fueled his lifelong interest in trying to understand and find solutions to overcome racism. When faced with a question that doesn't sound interesting to you, ask, "What would be a better question?" Even better: "What is the question that really interests me?"

Now, let's summarize the key insights from this chapter, and then take a moment to pause and reflect about your own level of interest.

Summary

- ✓ In order to serve stakeholders, leaders must understand their stakeholders' needs and what it takes to meet them.
- ✓ Human needs are served through the communities, organizations, systems and solutions we create.

✓ Understanding how these work and how they can be built to meet the needs of the stakeholders is absolutely critical for a leader.

✓ After caring and serving, understanding is the third of the seven essential leadership behaviors for creating positive change.

✓ While emotional empathy makes us care about others, and compassion commits us to serving them, interest is the key emotional driver to understanding human needs and the solutions that meet those needs.

✓ Together, empathy, compassion and interest build the foundation of the ASPIRE Leadership Model.

✓ Developing genuine interest in others, including their human needs and challenges, helps us transcend self-interest.

✓ Research shows that interest can be developed. The question is how?

✓ In order to develop interest:

- You want to be aware of who and what you need to be interested in.

- You should know what the barriers are to developing interest in that person and the solutions that serve that person's needs.

- You must then choose the right strategy and practice that helps you to overcome those barriers and develop interest.

Pause and Reflect

Before you begin reading the next chapter, I recommend pausing a moment to reflect: Think of your most challenging but critical stakeholder. This may be someone you rated low in your compassion test. Ask yourself, "Where am I with my ability to feel interested in the needs of this stakeholder and the solutions that would meet those needs?"

Interest in Their Needs:

1...2...3...4...5...6...7...8...9...10

Interest in the Solutions That Meet Their Needs:

1...2...3...4...5...6...7...8...9...10

For any of the two types of interest in which you are lower than seven, ask yourself:

- What is my biggest barrier? (See barriers above.)

- How could I overcome my biggest barrier? (See best practices above.)

- How will developing more interest in the needs and solutions allow me to understand better?

- How will understanding empower me to act differently toward that person?

- How might that change the person's behavior or actions?

Now that we have addressed the importance of understanding for a leader and how developing interest drives understanding, the next chapter will explore the importance of creating a vision and how the emotion of optimism provides the leader with a lens through which she sees future possibilities.

"If you are working on something exciting that you really care about, you don't have to be pushed. The vision pulls you."
~Steve Jobs

CHAPTER 4:
Optimism – The Lens for Visioning

The fourth essential behavioral competency for you as a leader, after caring, serving and understanding, is the ability to envision an aspirational new future for your stakeholders.

Envisioning a New Future

A vision aligned with your highest aspiration provides purpose and direction, which generate a deep and sustained commitment to act toward that vision. I experienced that when I joined Hewlett-Packard in Germany in the late 1980s. I was immediately assigned to a small task force to develop a proposal for a new software business. It was a time in which computing was starting to leave the data centers and spread out into the businesses and departments of the organizations. Our vision was to develop software that would allow information technology professionals to manage these highly distributed computing environments from one location. It was a new computing paradigm that needed innovative software to manage it.

At a coffee break outside our meeting room, Karl (name changed), a seasoned HP employee, introduced himself and asked me, "What are you working on?"

"I am helping to build a billion-dollar software business," I replied enthusiastically, without further explanation.

"Sorry, you are in the wrong company. We don't do software here," Karl answered and walked away.

He left me perplexed. At that moment, I didn't know why Karl had said that. Over time, I had many more conversations with longtime HP employees who expressed the same pessimism, even some senior executives who tried to stop HP's effort to start a software business. This was the '80s, when the software boom hadn't started, and there was no software company in the world that had reached a billion dollars in revenue yet. Like the other HP employees, Karl's career success had been built on developing hardware. Software was not what he knew and not what his company was known for. For him, the prospect of developing software probably seemed like playing in an unfamiliar field, and it may have not been aligned with his career aspirations. My colleagues and I, on the other hand, were working on a vision of a new future in software for HP that we believed in and that gave us purpose.

Past experience of success in one field can be a mental barrier to innovating in a new one. The reason is because to innovate, we have to think outside our mental box. For example, Karl's mental box was probably defined by his training and experience as a computer hardware engineer. Developing software may not have fit into that mental frame. Unlike Karl, although I had started my career in computer hardware, I had recognized the enormous possibilities of software.

My decision to move into building software proved to have been the right one.

When I retired from the company 24 years after my encounter with Karl, HP's software business had grown to more than $4 billion in yearly revenue, four times the amount I had blurted out to Karl. I had asserted a vision from my subconscious mind that he may not have seen as possible. At that moment, I had no idea how what I envisioned would happen, but I had committed to that endeavor because of my optimism that it was possible and because it gave me purpose. Without a sense of purpose and a belief that it was possible, I could not have committed as deeply and as long as I had. The vision pulled me forward.

The fourth essential behavioral competency for you as a leader, after caring, serving and understanding, is the ability to envision an aspirational new future for your stakeholders. When you create a vision that meets your stakeholders' highest aspirations, it provides a common purpose that pulls everybody forward.

That pull could also be observed with the East-German people who were drawn to demonstrate in the streets for "freedom and democracy" and in Daryl Davis, who persevered to change KKK members' belief system. A vision aligned with people's highest aspirations provides purpose and direction, which generate a deep and sustained commitment to act toward that vision.

While this appears to be straightforward, I often see organizational visions that are not only uninspiring, but the organization's employees don't even know what they are. I have observed two major reasons for this. One is lack of empathy, compassion and interest in the leaders who create these visions for their employees. This prevents them from caring about, committing to serve and understanding their needs. That's why the vision created doesn't align with what employees really care about. Think back to Jennifer, the executive in Chapter 1 who struggled to motivate her team and had failed to create such a vision. It was her lack of caring and interest in the needs of her team members that made her unable to understand their aspirations.

The second reason why leaders fail to envision a new aspirational future is that they find themselves in a deep crisis. That is the situation Chairman Heart, the Native American leader who you met in Chapter 1, found himself in when he was elected to become the chairman of his tribal council. The challenges his tribe faced included widespread poverty, homelessness, low life expectancy, mental health issues, high substance use, lack of education and career opportunities and suicide among young people. On a day-to-day basis, he and the other tribal leaders had to focus simply on helping people meet their basic needs for survival. It prevented them from thinking about the longer-term future.

Years later, as Chairman Heart reflected with me on the situation, he used a metaphor to describe how he felt about it. "If you are on a mountain on a clear day, you can see far and in all directions. But if you are down in a valley or in a ditch, you can't see far." Being in an organizational crisis like the one Chairman Heart and the tribal council found themselves in is like being in a ditch. He said, "We first had to climb out of it and onto a higher ground in order to see farther. That was my role as a leader." While the challenges of leading a tribe are unique, an existential crisis that poses a barrier to envisioning a better future for an organization or a community is a common challenge. The reason is that our emotional threat system is highly aroused when we are in an existential crisis. I will share more about that later in the barriers section.

Chairman Heart recognized the emotional valley he found himself in when he shared with me, "We are at risk of losing our children and, with that, our future." Realizing this, he decided to climb to higher ground in order to have a better vision of their future. He did this by hosting an offsite meeting where they articulated and, with the help of a visual artist, drew an image on a canvas of a future in which all the children, youth and families of the tribe would be healthy, safe and well. This vision was created by leaders who deeply care, are committed to serve and profoundly understand the needs and issues of their people. At that moment, they knew that they were far from making that vision a reality, but committing to such a purpose-driven vision created an emotional shift to optimism.

The tribe's new vision started a multi-year process in which it has made a lot of progress by executing strategies and plans developed along the way. As with any organization, while successful milestones can be reached, the work toward the vision is never finished, and if it is, a new vision must emerge to give people purpose and direction.

That is an important role of a leader. Chairman Heart and the members of the council followed this approach by stopping at major milestones along the way to take the opportunity to look back on what they had achieved, but also importantly to take a fresh look from the new plateau they had reached. From there they could see farther into the future, update their vision and set new goals.

Emotion for Envisioning a New Future

Empathy, compassion and interest build the emotional foundation for a leader to care, commit to serve and understand the needs of stakeholders. These emotions focus her energy on the present situation. For a leader to envision a better future, she needs to be in an emotional state that focuses her energy on the future, and that is optimism.

Optimism is the emotion associated with the belief that the outcome of something that you pursue will be positive. Lack of optimism will keep you from pursuing wholeheartedly the things in life that you desire, and it clouds the lens through which you see the future. That is why when a leader asks me to facilitate the creation of a new vision for her organization I assess how optimistic the people who are involved in that process are. If their optimism is too low, I try to focus on helping them develop optimism. The good news is that optimism can be learned, but before going into how, let me share about two types of optimism and how to apply each one.

Two Types of Optimism

Research distinguishes two types of optimism that are important for a leader to understand in order to fulfill his role of envisioning and leading others to an aspirational new future.

One type of optimism is associated with positive expectations about the future that are based on past experiences. That would explain why the tribal leaders were pessimistic about the possibilities in gaining real collaboration from the federal agencies. It had failed in the past. It would also explain why the seasoned HP employee told me I was in the wrong company for building a software business. He hadn't seen it done. Both the tribal leader's and the HP employee's past experiences prevented them from feeling optimistic about an aspirational new future in the areas I had discussed with them.

The second type of optimism comes from dreaming about something you desire to happen in the future despite the absence of any past evidence that it is possible. For example, imagine yourself dreaming about something you find highly desirable, such as living at your dream destination, being with someone you desire to be with or a dream job. Something you find highly desirable but unattainable, like some people's dream of winning the lottery. You fantasize about it, but deep down you believe that your wish for the future very likely won't become reality.

The question is what type of optimism do you need as a leader for creating a new aspirational future —the one rooted in past success or the type that comes from dreaming about the future despite the absence of any past evidence that the future is possible?

It depends on whether you are in the process of creating or pursuing the vision. In the process of creating a vision, you need to be able to think out of the box of your past experiences or current momentary situation. The type of optimism rooted in past experiences can keep your mind trapped in that box. This may be what happened with Karl, the HP employee when he said, "We don't do software here." He was likely in the mental box of developing "hardware." The type of optimism that allows you to dream helps you to think out-of-the-box and envision a new future. Once you have a clear vision and it comes to the question of how you are going to execute toward that vision, then the first type of optimism, grounded in practical experience of knowing how to execute, is helpful to create practical plans.

A process that I learned from my colleague Udaiyan Jatar applies the two types of optimism to the innovation process. Early in the process of our innovation workshops, we show our clients how to generate big new ideas that are not limited by their past experiences. That's when we cultivate the second type of optimism, i.e., dreaming of a new future outside the box of past experiences. Then when it comes to the question of how to execute toward that future, we guide participants in making a shift to the first type of optimism. That's the type that is fully aware of the barriers to make your big new ideas happen and also supports the creation of practical plans for executing toward your vision. Later in the "best practices" section, I will share more details about this approach.

Building on the foundation of caring, serving and understanding, the fourth essential behavioral competency for you as a leader is the ability to envision an aspirational new future for your stakeholders. While empathy, compassion and interest are the emotional drivers that make you care about and commit to serve and understand those needs, optimism allows you to see a new future where these are met, as illustrated below.

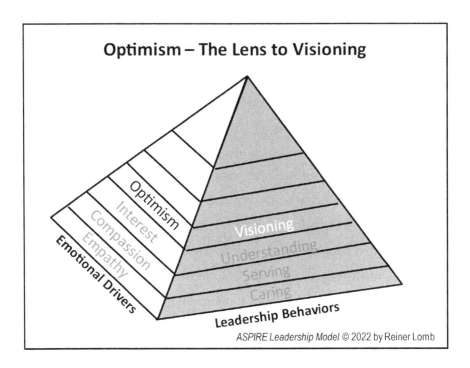

Optimism – The Lens to Visioning

Optimism

Interest

Compassion

Empathy

Emotional Drivers

Visioning

Understanding

Serving

Caring

Leadership Behaviors

ASPIRE Leadership Model © 2022 by Reiner Lomb

The good news is that optimism can be learned and developed. But as you have seen with Chairman Heart, who was first occupied with the survival of his tribe, there are barriers to optimism, which then also become barriers to envisioning and creating a new future. Before discussing the ways you can learn and develop optimism, let's take a look at the barriers to it. Knowing these will help you overcome them.

Barriers to Optimism

There are several barriers to optimism, which then become barriers to creating and pursuing the vision of an aspirational future. As a leader, knowing your barriers to optimism for creating and pursuing an aspirational future is absolutely critical in overcoming them. The two types of barriers to optimism to be aware of are negative thoughts and beliefs and the emotions associated with them. When these reinforce each other and become a vicious cycle, it may be hard to escape them without help from others.

Negative Thoughts and Beliefs

Barriers to optimism and to creating an aspirational future may include deeply held beliefs rooted in past experiences, such as "because the East German government crushed our demonstrations before, it will crush them again," or the HP employee's belief, "We don't do software here!" based on his past experience with the company.

Or such beliefs are part of our pessimistic thought patterns that may or may not be based on past experience, such as, "I don't deserve this," "I am not good or competent enough for this," "It will never work," or, "It is impossible." Beliefs such as these will affect our emotional state, so we might feel pessimistic, resigned or even depressed.

Emotional Barriers

In my work with leaders, I often notice emotions such as resentment, pessimism and resignation because of their perceived inability to change the situation. Those emotions, if they become a mood—a prolonged emotional state—become barriers to seeing and creating a possible future. They cloud or even cover the lens through which we see the world, the same way my pessimistic outlook on the future possibility of the Wall coming down clouded my lens to a future of a peaceful reunification for Germany.

The following are more detailed descriptions of emotional barriers and how to recognize them.

Pessimism and Resignation

When you feel pessimistic, your assessment may be that "regardless of my actions, the outcome will not be positive," and it makes you reluctant to act.

As a leader, you need to be conscious about when you express pessimism, even in ways you may not be aware of. For example, in a meeting, one of your team members shares an idea she is excited about, and you show disapproval by raising your eyebrow or shaking your head. Your team member's shoulders slump, and looking discouraged she drops back into her chair. It is then you can recognize the negative effect of your pessimism on the optimism of your team member.

When you feel resigned, your assessment may be that "there are very few opportunities for me, and I am unable to realize them," so you give up on taking action. For example, you notice resignation in a person when you hear them say, "I don't have hope," or, "I can't go on." Or you may see it in a resigned body posture.

While pessimism and resignation may be useful in *some* circumstances, such as opting *not* to go forward on a plan that may harm you or others, for you, the leader, pessimism and resignation are emotional barriers to seeing future possibilities.

Resentment

Resentment is an emotion associated with an assessment of the past. Its underlying story says, "I am a victim of someone's unjust action," and, "I have the moral right to or deserve something better." The resentment you feel could be targeted at a person, a group or a whole class of people, as we have experienced with political leaders around the world who want to gain and secure power, so they fire up resentment among their supporters against other groups.

The emotional state of resentment is close to anger, with the difference that anger is expressed outwardly and resentment is hidden. That makes it difficult to recognize and acknowledge it.

I observe that people who are in a state of resentment for a longer time suffer enormously without being aware that it is generated by a story that replays in the back of their mind. Replaying the injustice a person perceived he experienced keeps him mentally and emotionally stuck in the past. He has no mental energy left to focus on the future. Therefore, envisioning a new and better future is impossible.

Feeling Helpless, Worthless, Low Self-Confidence

When someone feels helpless, the assessment may be, "I am incapable of doing this myself." Research shows that people who feel helpless believe that their actions will be futile or nothing they do matters. They also blame their failure on lack of ability and worthlessness. This suggests low self-confidence and low self-esteem as emotional barriers to optimism. I observe that when a person is assessing a problem as too big to solve, what it often means is that the problem is too big to be solved alone. What someone really needs in this situation is to seek help.

Not Daring to Pursue Big Dreams

Then there is the fear of pursuing big dreams. That means, "I believe this is too big and risky to pursue, and it will make me fail. So I'd better stop dreaming big!"

Sometimes multiple emotional barriers overlap. Pessimism, feeling helpless, low confidence and not daring to pursue big dreams can all compound to prevent you from pursuing a new future you dream about.

Now let's look at some of the best practices for overcoming these barriers and for developing optimism.

Developing Optimism: Best Practices

As described earlier in this chapter, there are two types of optimism: positive expectations about the future that are based on past experiences and the more free-flowing thoughts and images that are rooted in wishes and desires despite the absence of any past experience that something will be possible.

First, we'll start with an exercise that helps you develop optimism that is rooted in wishes and desires, which is a must for visionary leaders. Then the next three exercises will help you overcome barriers to optimism.

Dream Big

This exercise (from Udaiyan Jatar) begins with choosing a key stakeholder or group of stakeholders you care about and are committed to serving. Then reflect on their highest aspirations, an unmet human need or an issue that you are passionate about solving. Now, with a realistic timeframe in mind, imagine the ideal or best possible future for this group of people in which that need was perfectly satisfied. Make the images as vivid as possible by describing how the people for whom you create the vision will live, act and behave in their ideal future.

For example, Klaus, a political activist from Germany in his late 60s, shared with me his dream of a society in which all people in the world live in solidarity with each other and not at the expense of future generations. When I asked him to be more specific, he envisioned that all our energy needs will be satisfied through renewable energy sources such as solar or wind power to prevent further global warming. He also dreamed about people around the world solving conflicts peacefully and living and working in solidarity with each other. He pointed out that in his vision, people have learned and practiced balancing their own interests with the interests of others.

I again asked him to be more specific, and he explained, "If there is a conflict between someone's own interest and that of others, those in conflict with each other find a compromise peacefully." Klaus dared to dream big before assessing whether his vision was realistic or not, and he was able to describe the new behaviors of the people for whom he envisioned a new future.

To ground his vision in a deeper purpose, I asked him why this vision was important to him. He replied, "Growing up in West Germany after World War II, I was pained when I learned about the crimes of the Nazi regime. I saw the horrible pictures of the concentration camps, and I was angry when I learned how complicit my parents' generation was." For Klaus, this painful experience motivated his lifelong activism.

In this exercise, I ask you to do the same for your key stakeholders. You are practicing the second type of optimism, based on wishes and desires. You are dreaming of a future as if there were no limitations and then asking yourself why it is that important to you.

Once you have envisioned your stakeholders' ideal future and how their behavior would have to change to make your vision a reality, the next exercise is designed to shift to the first type of optimism, which is more grounded in reality. This second exercise, mental contrasting, helps you become aware of the barriers to your vision and identify ways to overcome them.

Mental Contrasting

Thinking about what stands in the way of making your vision a reality is called mental contrasting. Research by Gabriele Oettingen shows that juxtaposing the future you dream about with potential obstacles triggers the energy needed to overcome the identified obstacles. It will motivate you to take actions toward your desired future because your subconscious mind will find ways of overcoming your barriers and increase the likelihood of making it happen. The following approach (from Udaiyan Jatar) designed to assist you in that process uses a form of mental contrasting.

First, with your vision of an ideal future for your key stakeholders and their desired behavior in mind, ask yourself, "What are the barriers that keep this person from changing to the desired behavior?" For example, Klaus identified as a barrier people's belief that succeeding in life means achieving financial success and gaining power over others. Associated with that belief, he also identified "win-lose" thinking, meaning that if others win in regard to those achievements, I lose, which is a barrier to helpful solutions when a conflict of interest arises. Klaus also added a fear of failing as an emotional barrier to people's changing their behavior.

Second, once you're aware of the desired behaviors and the barriers, reflect on what it would take to overcome these barriers. For example, for Klaus to overcome the barriers to his vision, he came up with ideas for changes in the education of children and young people about what success in life really means. He emphasized the importance of success for everyone, which means valuing win-win thinking. Klaus also conceived of self-awareness practices like meditation that can help overcome a person's focus on themselves or the ego. Identifying these as practical solutions made him feel more optimistic, and that motivated him to act on his dream.

Dispute Negative Beliefs and Thoughts

It is possible to overcome negative beliefs and thought patterns by disputing them. You can do this by questioning their accuracy, reflecting on all possible contributing causes to what happened, de-catastrophizing the situation or asking about the usefulness of dwelling on your negative thoughts. For example, you may dispute a belief, such as, "I can never do that because I tried once and failed," by recognizing that it is factually incorrect. Daryl Davis used the approach of disputing, "They hate me," by asking, "How can they hate me if they don't even know me?" This is what allowed him to engage with the KKK members and eventually influence them to change their belief about Black people.

Overcome Resentment

Resentment is associated with negative thoughts of being a victim of someone's actions. Thought patterns associated with resentment hold your brain hostage because you are constantly struggling with the injustice that happened to you. If not changed, resentment will become your mood, and you may slip into anger or resignation. In the state of resentment, you won't be able to focus on the future and on creating a vision. In order to shift from resentment to optimism, you first must accept what happened to you is something that is in the past, that you cannot change because it happened already. You don't have to like what happened. You just have to accept it as something you cannot change and therefore will not spend any emotional energy on. Now, freed from repeated negative thoughts about the past, you can shift to thinking about possibilities for the future. The following example shows the power of such an emotional shift.

One day at work, my manager and I were called in for an unexpected meeting with our general manager, who told us, "I have to put the software engineers I had committed to you on another project." Then he went on to explain that he needed them for another project that was more strategic than the one I had been spearheading. I glanced briefly at my manager, who was sitting next to me. Like me, he was caught off guard by the bad news.

In that moment, I felt resentment toward the general manager. I had worked hard for nearly two years on this project, researching the customer needs and the market, writing the business plan and working with the engineering team to plan the development of the new product. The actual software development was just about to begin. I was deeply invested emotionally, and I was convinced this product would be a success. However, as soon as this meeting was over, my manager and I would then have to announce to the team that the project was canceled. At that point, I could have easily stayed in resentment. But I realized that the decision had been made, and I could not change it. I knew then that the best way forward for me was to accept the decision so I could focus my energy on what I could change, the future, and I did just that.

When I sensed that the GM was about to get up from his chair, I asked, "Can we just have one more moment?" The GM nodded. "I believe we can pull the project off without our own developers if we could just keep a couple of people from the engineering team on this project," I told him. The GM wanted to know more about my idea. I explained that the product plan and specifications had been finalized and that we would only need to find an external software development partner company that would develop the product according to our specifications. My manager chimed in to support the idea. The GM agreed. I was relieved, although we didn't know yet if and where to find such a company.

Fortunately, only a few months after the meeting, we found a suitable external software development partner, and we signed a software development contract. About a year later, we launched the product globally, and it kept growing rapidly year after year. Nearly two decades after we had launched the product, it was still one of the top-selling software products at HP. Had I not shifted out of resentment at that crucial moment by accepting the decision to pull the resources from my project, it would have prevented me from focusing my energy on thinking about new possibilities to develop the product, and it might never have happened.

Acceptance is a gateway to optimism because it allows you to stop focusing your mental energy what you cannot change, and start focusing on what you can change—the future. Let me be clear, accepting in this case does not mean that you have to like what happened or give up on your vision. I didn't like the decision of the GM, but I didn't give up on my vision to produce and launch the software product I had planned.

Acceptance in this case means, "I acknowledge that an action was taken that I don't like, but I cannot undo it. Because I cannot undo what happened in the past, I decided to not spend mental energy on rehashing the past." With that acceptance, I have shifted away from resentment toward creating new possibilities for the future. This may include correcting the wrongdoings toward me, for example, by ending a relationship with someone who mistreated me. That decision is an action that comes out of thinking about future possibilities, not by rehashing the past.

Now let's summarize the key learnings about the fourth essential leadership behavior for creating change: envisioning a new future and the two types of optimism that will help you as a leader in that process.

Summary:

- ✓ A vision aligned with people's highest aspirations provides *purpose, direction* and generates a *deep and sustained commitment* to act toward that vision.

- ✓ To be a visionary leader, you must first imagine an aspirational future for your stakeholders, and second, you must be able to bring it to fruition.

- ✓ This requires two different types of optimism.

- ✓ The first type of optimism allows you to dream big without limitations.

- ✓ The second type of optimism is grounded in reality and uses mental contrasting to identify barriers to your vision, and your subconscious mind will find ways of overcoming them.

- ✓ Both types of optimism can be learned by identifying your barriers and choosing the right practice.

Pause and Reflect

Before you continue reading, I recommend pausing a moment and reflecting:

- Who are my most critical stakeholders?

- What are their aspirational needs?

- What is my vision for the future in which their aspirational needs are met?

- How optimistic am I that I can create that future?

Optimism:

1...2...3...4...5...6...7...8...9...10

If your optimism is lower than eight, ask yourself, "What are the biggest barriers to creating the future I envision?" Depending on what your biggest barriers are, you may revisit the exercises above now or later.

Now that we have addressed the importance for a leader to envision an aspirational new future for her stakeholders and how the emotion of optimism provides a lens for focusing on the future, the next chapter will explore the importance of mobilizing people toward the leader's vision and how inspiration energizes people.

"Action without vision is only passing time; vision without action is merely daydreaming, but vision with action can change the world."
– Nelson Mandela

CHAPTER 5:
Inspiration – The Energy for Mobilizing

Vision Without Acting Is Merely Daydreaming

The previous chapter addressed the importance for a leader of envisioning an aspirational new future. Making that vision a reality requires action. Without it, you are merely daydreaming, which, while it is a pleasant distraction, does not automatically lead to action. That's why you want to mobilize your stakeholders to act toward your vision.

Mobilizing is the fifth of the seven essential behavioral leadership competencies. It builds on the previous four: caring, which is awakened by feeling empathy; the commitment to serving, which comes from feeling compassion; understanding, which develops through interest; and visioning, which is powered by optimism. In the same way that emotions fuel the previous four leadership behaviors, they also fuel mobilizing people to act. Let's explore this more with the following example.

When I first talked to Jennifer, who you met in Chapter 1, she confided that she feared she wouldn't reach the ambitious goals management had set for her department. She was afraid of failing and blamed it on her team's lack of motivation. When I asked why she believed the team wasn't motivated, she told me, "They are all lazy!" She believed her team members should be motivated to give their best because they were paid well. Rationally, that makes sense. Jennifer wasn't yet aware that a primary driver of employee engagement is the emotions people feel related to their work or the workplace. Research shows that emotions are 400% more powerful than rational reasons in energizing and mobilizing people to give their very best. This means that an employee who is emotionally motivated puts in four times the effort of one motivated only by such reasons as pay or benefits.

The leader plays an essential role in energizing people. According to Gallup, leaders account for 70% of effective employee engagement. Unaware of her part in this essential role, Jennifer, because she felt helpless, blamed her team and used anger and threats to try to motivate them. This backfired because it depressed the team's morale even more, and they responded with resentment and distrust, emotions that took the energy that they needed to achieve their goals. The old carrot-and-stick method had failed.

Before Jennifer could learn how to mobilize her team, she needed to understand that it wasn't laziness that demotivated them, but her leadership behaviors. I guided her through an empathy exercise that allowed her to feel the effect of her own behavior. Once she came to understand this and recognize how essential her own behavior was in mobilizing others, she felt motivated to learn and practice new leadership behaviors.

The question I next explored with Jennifer was if emotions such as fear or anger failed to motivate her team, what emotion would be most effective in mobilizing them to act toward their goals? The answer is inspiration. In fact, research by Zenger/Folkman shows that the ability to inspire is the most powerful leadership competency that distinguishes extraordinary leaders from all others. It's an ability that engages people's hearts, not just their minds. Let's now explore inspiration in more detail, what it looks like when a leader inspires, what its barriers are and practices you can use to inspire.

Inspiration – The Emotion That Mobilizes People

Traci is a leader who wants to mobilize different stakeholders to make her vision a reality. She is the founder and CEO of Apto Global, a software company whose vision it is to allow those who are going to relocate or travel to a foreign country to immerse themselves virtually from home in that new culture and language.

This can help them feel more at home when they arrive and succeed in their new environment. It's an ambitious vision, born out of her passion for languages and diverse cultures, and her aspiration for people to flourish in a diverse world.

To make her vision a reality, she needed to mobilize various types of stakeholders, including investors, employees and contractors with different types of expertise, such as software developers, marketing experts, salespeople and, most importantly, clients to buy and use her product. As I watched Traci attract people to invest in or join Apto, I observed in her a natural ability to inspire.

One example was Ken (name changed), an experienced professional who initially was hesitant about joining Apto because he wasn't sure if working in a startup would be a good fit for him. However, after he talked to Traci, he felt inspired because she was able to connect Apto's vision to Ken's experience in working and living in different countries. He had gone through the pain of relocating to a foreign country without speaking the language or knowing much of the culture. Traci's vision of allowing people to immerse themselves in the culture and language virtually beforehand inspired Ken.

Inspiration engages people's hearts, which makes them actually look forward to and become totally absorbed in their work. In these instances, people feel fulfilled and perform at their best. When people are inspired, they approach their work with more optimism, creativity and self-esteem. In short,

Inspiration is a motivational state that compels individuals to bring ideas into fruition.

You may recognize the difference when you are served by an emotionally engaged client representative of a company. While one person might mechanically process your request, another one—without even being asked—goes out of her way to solve your problem. That's the difference between an inspired and an uninspired employee.

Emotional psychology describes three characteristics of inspiration.

Evocation: Inspiration is evoked in someone rather than voluntarily chosen by them. Ken was initially hesitant to join Traci's startup, but when she shared her vision, he felt inspired. As a former expat who learned the hard way how to succeed in a new culture, Ken realized that if he had been able to immerse himself virtually in that culture before moving there, he would have felt more at home from the beginning. Traci's vision for Apto evoked inspiration in Ken because he was able to envision helping thousands of people make this same transition more easily.

Transcendence: This is the awareness of new possibilities that goes above ordinary or mundane concerns. Because Ken had initially struggled living and working in a culture and language different from his own, he connected with the purpose of helping people succeed and flourish in the foreign country they relocated to. In that way, Traci's and Ken's purpose aligned.

Approach Motivation: Motivates someone to transmit, actualize or express a new vision, such as Traci's vision that allows people to virtually immerse themselves into a new culture and language before they relocate. Traci's vision inspired Ken to help her make it happen.

I will come back to these three characteristics in the section about how you can learn to inspire your stakeholders.

To create the future you envision, you want to mobilize people to act toward it, and to mobilize them, you need to inspire them. After *caring, serving, understanding and visioning* that were covered in Chapters 1–4, *mobilizing* people toward your vision is the next essential leadership behavior for bringing it to fruition. Inspiration is the emotion that builds on empathy, compassion, interest and optimism to mobilize people, as illustrated in the image below.

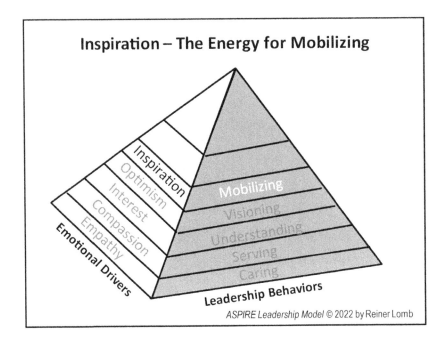

Inspiration – The Energy for Mobilizing

Inspiration

Optimism

Interest

Compassion

Empathy

Emotional Drivers

Mobilizing

Visioning

Understanding

Serving

Caring

Leadership Behaviors

ASPIRE Leadership Model © 2022 by Reiner Lomb

Before sharing best practices for how you can learn to inspire people you want to mobilize, let's look at some of the main barriers to it.

Barriers to Inspiration

Following is a list of leadership behaviors that are barriers to inspiration.

Failing to Connect to a Purpose

While most organizations have a vision and mission statement, very few people in organizations can connect their role and the work they're doing to a purpose that inspires them. One major reason I have observed is that their individual aspirations—what they care about—are not aligned with the vision and mission of the organization. Leaders who overlook the vital step of connecting the organization's purpose with employees' higher aspirations fail to inspire them. Traci in the earlier example was able to help Ken make that connection. He became inspired by Traci's purpose because it aligned with his own aspirations.

The other major reason is that leaders do not clarify how each person's contribution brings the organization's vision and mission to life. Employees feel uninspired when they don't see a connection between their daily work and a purpose they care about. In Ken's case, this means that although he is aligned with Apto's purpose, he also needs to see how his role in the company will contribute to this purpose.

Setting Goals That Are Not Challenging or Don't Seem Achievable

Inspiring leaders provide a clear sense of purpose, but they also set goals that mark significant achievements in fulfilling that purpose. Those leaders who are simply setting goals that are not challenging enough miss out on this powerful tool for inspiring those whom they lead. As a result, people are uninspired to perform. Can you imagine Tom Brady, the football quarterback who won seven Super Bowls, feeling inspired to join a team that sets a season goal to come in second? The same is true for the people you are leading. If you set goals that are beneath their capabilities, they may feel uninspired to perform their best.

However, there is a fine balance to this. When setting ambitious goals, it's best to create the conditions in which these goals are achievable with people's best efforts. Setting goals that people feel are not achievable, no matter how hard or creatively they work, also becomes a barrier to their feeling inspired.

Lacking Energy and Enthusiasm

When a leader lacks energy and enthusiasm in how he shows up, it can drain the energy of the whole team. When this occurs for a sustained time, the mood of the team may become apathetic, which is the feeling of being uninspired to take action. An example is Walter (name changed), who was promoted to a new management position. He was motivated by the status and the higher pay, but he himself was not enthusiastic about the mission of his organization. Whenever Walter communicated with his team, it was without energy or enthusiasm, and it drained the energy of everyone in the room. As a result, people felt uninspired to engage and act.

Not Supporting People in Their Personal Development

A leader who is known for developing people and helping them pursue and achieve their career aspirations will attract, retain and engage talented people. A lack of such support for employees' development, such as not having a personal development plan, no alignment of their work with their career aspirations, or lack of coaching or mentoring will leave them uninspired to support the leader and perform at their best.

When it comes to coaching and mentoring, leaders who don't take an interest in helping others develop new skills or capabilities so they can perform and grow lack the inspiration that people need to thrive. When a manager doesn't give regular and helpful feedback, employees are left in the dark about how their performance is perceived and what they did well or need to improve. It creates a feeling of uncertainty about where they stand in the eyes of their manager and the direction for their personal development. That uncertainty may even fuel anxiety and fear. Not coaching, mentoring or even giving regular feedback sends the message to employees that they are not important, and they feel unappreciated and unvalued. Lack of coaching or mentoring is a barrier to inspiration.

Lack of Interest in Ideas or Input

Lack of interest in an employee's ideas suffocates any possibility for inspiring that person. Leaders who never ask for input and suggestions or, worse, discourage the involvement of the group fail to bring out the best in their employees. I was once hired by an organization to help its employees develop more innovative behaviors, such as creating and sharing ideas. Yet when I interviewed the employees, they complained that whenever they brought their ideas to the executives, they didn't show much interest or even dismissed them outright. As a result, the employees felt discouraged from innovating.

Perception That Important Information Is Not Shared

People sense when a leader is withholding important information. They may notice subtle changes in a leader's behavior, such as hesitating to answer questions, and later learn that important information was not shared with them or shared too late.

There are several reasons why leaders may not share important information, including an attempt to gain or maintain power, lack of awareness that other people would truly benefit, being too absorbed in their own work to take the time or a fear that giving too much information or sharing it too early may distract people unnecessarily from their work.

When employees sense that important information is being withheld from them, they often feel disconnected from what's going on in the company or even distrustful of the leader. People need access to information to inform their own work decisions. Without that, they are set up for failure. Feeling disconnected, distrust and not being set up for success are all barriers to inspiration.

Not Walking the Talk

Employees quickly recognize when leaders don't walk their talk, meaning that they say one thing but do another. Imagine that a leader set a new goal, and you signed up to support it and then learned he has done something in conflict with the pursuit of this goal. You now feel betrayed and used. In the company for which a coaching client of mine worked, the CEO had given a speech to the employees in which he asked them to support his cost-cutting goals. My client's team members were initially supportive until they learned that the CEO himself appeared to still spend lavishly. The people on my client's team expressed their frustration, and my client had a hard time inspiring them to support the CEO's cost-cutting goals.

The previous list of barriers aims to help you assess what behaviors of your own you may want to focus on when developing your ability to inspire. Take a moment to reflect on the list and identify the ones that may be your greatest barriers. Next, you will learn about some best practices for developing inspiration. Keep your barriers to inspiration in mind when you read this section.

Developing Inspiration: Best Practices

Mobilizing people to support the change you aspire to will require you to anticipate how your different stakeholders feel about that change. There are some who will feel enthusiastic when you share your vision, and they will be ready to sign up and join you. They are the easiest to inspire. There will be a second, often larger group who are often referred to as the majority, who initially will feel apathetic about your vision because they may not see a connection to their own aspirations. That's why they are harder to inspire than the enthusiasts. Last, there will be a third group of those who feel skeptical or even threatened by the change you want to create, and when they hear about it, some may even try to stop you. I suggest that you focus on the enthusiasts first, and when they are mobilized, maximize their help to mobilize the second group, the ones who feel apathetic. Once you have the majority mobilized, it will be much harder for the third group to stop you because of the momentum you have created.

Remember the example of the Monday Demonstrators, who created the peaceful revolution that brought down the Berlin Wall. These demonstrations started with only a small group of people on Sept 4, 1989, who then inspired more and more people to join, growing week after week to 70,000, 120,000 and then to 320,000 by October 23 in a city of only 500,000 people. Once the demonstrations had reached that enormous size, they were hard to stop.

This example may sound daunting when you think about how to apply this process to your leadership role because of the huge risk people took and the numbers involved. However, these steps for creating change involve the same essential behavioral and emotional competencies applied by many changemakers around the world. They all started small and then, step by step, scaled the number of people they mobilized. They were mobilized because they were inspired by the leaders' vision—in the case of the Monday Demonstrators, the vision of freedom. Now let's look at some of the behaviors you can apply to inspire people, starting with the importance of the vision itself.

Connect to Purpose

You want to inspire people because you want to mobilize them to act toward making your vision a reality. In Chapter 4, I shared how to create a vision aligned with people's highest aspirations. Such a vision provides *purpose, direction* and generates a *deep and sustained commitment* for the people you want to mobilize to act toward that vision.

Now the vital step for inspiring them is to help people see the connection between your team's or organization's purpose and their own aspirations in life. Traci in the earlier example was able to help Ken make that connection. He became inspired by Apto's purpose because it aligned with his own aspirations.

Once people feel inspired to join you in your efforts, a second important step is to clarify how this person's contribution brings the organization's vision and mission to life. In Ken's case, although he was aligned with Apto's purpose, Traci also needed to help Ken see how his work in the company contributed to this purpose.

Communicate with Enthusiasm

Emotions are contagious and communicating your vision with enthusiasm, exuding passion and energy, will create an emotional resonance with your audience. People will feel more inspired when they see the spark in your eyes and your confident posture and gestures of excitement. Juergen Klopp, the team manager of the

Liverpool F.C., is a great example of someone who inspires his team and its fans by showing great enthusiasm and passion with his whole body from the sidelines. While sport seems to be a natural place for using physical expressions to inspire, this benefit is not limited to sports. I have watched the audience sit seemingly disengaged when the CFO of their company entered the room for his yearly financial report. As he began shuffling his papers around and started to speak, people sat in apathy. Then, as he progressed in presenting his company's numbers, he became more and more animated, enthusiastic and passionate, and when he finished, the audience erupted in a standing ovation that lasted long after he had left the podium. These are examples in which the leaders evoked inspiration in others. You can do this by acting and sounding enthusiastic yourself while connecting with others in the room, including making eye contact.

Compassionate Support

You can create positive one-on-one relationships along with team relationships by being a great listener, taking interest in the needs and ideas people have and connecting emotionally. One example is the practice of managing by wandering around (MBWA), which is an informal and unscheduled way to walk through the workplace, checking in and taking an empathetic interest in people's work, understanding the challenges they might have but also listening to and understanding people's needs for growth. Then you support them in their development and overcoming their challenges through coaching and mentoring. This is also an opportunity to share your vision and show real interest in people's ideas and acknowledge their contributions.

At Hewlett-Packard, MBWA was encouraged through an open-door policy, not just for managers but for any employee. I have continued this practice even in a virtual work environment by informally checking in with people randomly via text messaging, phone or video calls. When people work remotely, it becomes even more important to connect in these ways so that people don't feel isolated. I encourage you to find your own approach to supporting people in a compassionate way. When you do, it will inspire them to act toward your vision and goals.

Setting Challenging Enough Goals

Setting challenging enough yet achievable goals helps to overcome apathy and to inspire. There is a fine balance to setting goals that are both challenging and achievable at the same time. When you are setting ambitious goals, it is critical to also create the conditions in which, with people's best effort, these goals are achievable. Examples are setting challenging yet achievable quarterly targets for all major aspects of the business, such as sales, operations, team development or innovation.

Role Model Living up to Values

Provide a powerful role model of doing the right things in the right way. This behavior helps to overcome distrust. This goes back to the earlier example about the CEO who asked everybody in his company to cut costs but continued to spend lavishly. In order to inspire people, he would have to model living up to what he asked everybody else to do, for example, by demonstrating how he has been decreasing his own company related spending.

Sharing Expertise and Knowledge

Provide direction that comes from a deep expertise and knowledge. This behavior helps others to see new possibilities for acting toward their goals. For example, in my third year of studying computer science at my university, I felt nervous when I attended my first class with Logan (name changed), a newly hired professor who was teaching a new field of computer science in which he was one of the world's leading experts. I feared that his class would be too difficult for me to follow, but at the same time I really wanted to take the class because of his deep expertise.

On the morning of my first class, I watched Logan enter the seminar room, greet us with a friendly and open smile and share what we could expect from his class. As he started his first lecture, I was in awe of how he was developing a very complex topic step by step using metaphors, examples from other fields of science and other useful tools to make the topic understandable. He took us on a journey that opened my eyes to a whole new world of designing computers for the future. I felt thrilled when that first class ended.

I had finally found a professor who shared his deep expertise in a way that inspired me to want to learn more. And I did. Later I chose his field as the topic of my research for my master's thesis. This is an example of how sharing expertise and knowledge in a way that makes it accessible to others helps to inspire people.

Connecting to a higher purpose has both the potential to evoke inspiration in someone and to create an awareness of new possibilities that transcend ordinary concerns, two of the characteristics of inspiration. Compassionate support, setting appropriate goals, role modeling values and sharing expertise are all behaviors that help with approach motivation, the third characteristic of inspiration, i.e., they motivate someone to transmit, actualize or express the new vision.

Three Leaders, Three Different Approaches to Inspiration

Behaviors for inspiring others can be learned, no matter your personality, charisma or personal style. The following examples come from my own experiences with three leaders who greatly inspired me, each of whom practices a different combination of the behaviors shared above. I have substituted different names for each of them.

Expertise, Enthusiasm and Compassionate Support

Building on Logan's example, in addition to making his deep expertise accessible in creative ways, he used two other inspiring behaviors. One was the enthusiasm with which he taught us. From the moment he entered the room, he had a spark in his eyes and a smile on his face, and he gestured with excitement as he spoke and drew on the white board. He kept us captivated by maintaining eye contact and interacting with us. When he sensed that he'd lost us, he stopped immediately and tried to explain in a different way. For Logan, there was no stupid question. This gave me courage to ask whatever I wanted to. He always stayed positive and encouraging in his response.

His expertise in his field and how he made it accessible to us made me want to know more. I took advantage of the time he made himself available at his office, asked questions, read the research papers he suggested and finally chose his research field for my master's thesis. Although I was not planning an academic career, I was so inspired that I even joined a newly created lab focused on Logan's field of research. In all my interactions with him, he was not only a great listener but also connected with me emotionally during our conversations. For example, when I came to his office for advice, he would stand up from his chair behind the desk, pull another chair over and gesture for me to sit down. Then he would take a moment to connect with me as a person, not just as a student, by asking how I was doing. I felt genuinely appreciated as a human being, interested student and potential research colleague.

Decades later, I still feel inspired by his behaviors and try to model them when I interact with people, such as being enthusiastic, generously sharing expertise and showing support.

Compassionate Support and Being a Role Model

In one of my roles at Hewlett-Packard, my manager Oscar (name changed) gave me a great deal of autonomy in my work. Yet whenever I walked into his office and asked him for his help with a challenge, he would immediately stop what he was doing and listen attentively and empathetically. During these meetings, he made an effort to understand the issue and was a great sounding board for my ideas. I typically left inspired and confident to act on the issue that I had come to him to help me think through.

But most remarkable to me was how Oscar served as a role model when working across departments, despite the attitudes of some of the other department heads. For example, during the yearly budget planning, Greg, the head of another department, tried to boost his budget allocation without considering the needs of the other departments. Oscar argued for an allocation that was balanced and helped the organization as a whole meet its goals. Because Oscar's leadership behavior was not driven by "silo thinking" the way that Greg's was, he gained the trust of people across the organization. He truly stands out as a leader who modeled prioritizing the success of the organization over selfish needs and provided me with autonomy in my decision making while also offering support when I needed it.

Vision, Challenging Goals and Enthusiasm

Adrian had just been hired to lead a newly formed global sales organization. I attended my first meeting with him as a guest and sitting in the midst of the people from his organization. Adrian spoke from the front of the room, standing and walking close to the front row and making eye contact with everyone in the room. He shared a big vision and aspirational goals for the organization. His voice was filled with enthusiasm, and his gestures energetically supported his words. At one point, he drew a steep line on a flip chart and added numbers that showed the goals for the organization over time. Then he made a connection between his aspirational goals for the organization and the potential for career growth of each individual in the room associated with these goals.

Adrian inspired people by connecting their aspirations with the vision and goals of the organization, and he did it with irresistible enthusiasm. When he was finished, people got up and started to mingle. When I joined their conversations, I could hear how inspired they felt. I felt inspired too, and that is what mobilized me to apply for and accept an open leadership position on his team.

The ability to inspire is the most powerful leadership competency that distinguishes extraordinary leaders. It is an ability that engages hearts, not just minds. These three leaders definitely engaged my heart. As I described before, negative emotions mobilize a destructive energy. The leaders who have inspired me mobilized a creative energy.

These three leaders inspired through a combination of behaviors that fit their individual style. You may want to reflect for a moment on which of the previous inspiring behaviors fit your style best, and then practice those on a regular basis and see how people react. Even focusing on only one or two of those practices will make you a more inspiring leader. I encourage you to develop and practice your own style to inspire.

Let's summarize the key learnings about the fifth essential leadership competency of inspiring and mobilizing people.

Summary:

- ✓ To create the future you envision, you need to mobilize people.
- ✓ Inspiration is the emotion that mobilizes people to act.
- ✓ The ability to inspire is the most powerful leadership competency that distinguishes extraordinary leaders.
- ✓ Behaviors that inspire people can be learned and developed.
- ✓ Gain clarity about the stakeholders you want to mobilize and in what order.
- ✓ Identify your barriers to inspiration.
- ✓ Identify and practice a set of inspiring behaviors that fit your style and help overcome your barriers to inspiration
- ✓ Most importantly, connect your vision to people's highest aspirations, and communicate it with enthusiasm.

Pause and Reflect

Before you continue reading, I recommend that you pause and reflect a moment about which person in your life inspired you most. Consider people from your earliest childhood all the way to today. Try to remember that person as vividly as you can. This can be someone who you have personally met or you have learned about in other ways, such as through reading or film. I became inspired by Nelson Mandela's leadership behaviors when I read his autobiography, *Long Walk to Freedom*. What I found inspiring was how Mandela role modeled compassion for his white guards despite them representing the apartheid government that put him in prison. He continued that compassionate behavior toward both Black and white South Africans as the first Black president of South Africa.

- Who inspired you?
- What were the behaviors that inspired you?
- How has that affected your life?
- Which of those behaviors fit your style to inspire others?

Next, think about your most critical stakeholder(s) and ask yourself, "How inspired are they to support me in making my vision a reality?"

Inspiration:

1...2...3...4...5...6...7...8...9...10

If your or your key stakeholders' inspiration is lower than 8, ask yourself:

- What are my biggest barriers to inspiring them?
- What are the behaviors that best fit my style and overcome my barriers?

Now that we have addressed the importance for a leader of mobilizing people and how the emotion of inspiration provides the energy for mobilizing, the next chapter will explore the importance of achieving collaboration and how trust fuels collaboration.

"Trust is the glue of life. It's the most essential ingredient in effective communication. It's the foundational principle that holds all relationships."
~Stephen Covey

CHAPTER 6:
Trust – The Fuel for Collaborating

Once you have mobilized the right people to support your vision, the sixth essential leadership behavior is to coordinate effective actions. You do this by setting measurable goals, creating action plans and assigning roles and responsibilities for executing your plans. This is as true for executing toward a vision of societal change such as freedom and democracy as it is for an organizational change such as creating a new software business. In both examples I shared earlier—the East German Revolution and the creation of a software business—after people were mobilized, it was time to coordinate actions.

Let's take another look at the Monday Demonstrations in Leipzig in 1989. Two young pastors, Christian Fuehrer and Christoph

Wonneberg, needed to organize the demonstrations. It took planning and coordination to hold the peace prayers, to motivate people to attend and then to demonstrate afterward. They had to agree to voice their demands peacefully, even in the face of police scare tactics, provocations and violence. To make their demands heard, they had to assemble at the same place at the same time and walk together in the same direction. They also had to agree on their response to possible police violence, practicing non-violence. Actions like these required close collaboration. The demonstrations started with a small group who then inspired more and more people to join, growing within only a few weeks to an astonishing crowd of 320,000.

In a similar way, to create a new software business, my colleagues and I at HP needed to agree on strategies, set goals, create action plans, define roles and responsibilities and then execute in a coordinated way. This, too, required close collaboration.

Collaboration is the sixth of the seven essential behavioral leadership competencies. It builds on the previous five: caring, which is awakened by feeling empathy; the commitment to serving, which comes from feeling compassion; understanding, which develops through interest; visioning, which is powered by optimism; and mobilizing, which comes from feeling inspired to act. Like the previous five leadership behaviors, collaboration is also driven by an emotion, and that emotion is trust. Lack of trust, on the other hand, hinders collaboration.

Trust is at the heart of leadership because it affects every single one of the seven leadership behaviors and associated emotional drivers discussed in this book. That's why trust is the sixth of the seven essential emotions for leading change, and research shows that high-trust organizations perform better and have healthier, happier and more engaged employees. Before I explain these correlations in more detail, let me share the following example that gives a deeper insight into the power of trust.

Trust Sealed the Deal

Helmut Kohl, chancellor of West Germany at the time of the fall of the Wall, wanted to use the momentum of the mobilization of the people in East Germany to reunify the country. To achieve that, he first had to overcome the distrust of the leaders of France, the UK and the USA, who would have to agree, but most importantly, he needed to gain the trust of the leader of the Soviet Union, Mikhail Gorbachev.

Unfortunately for Kohl, the two men had gotten off to a bad start in their relationship after Gorbachev had become the general secretary of the Communist Party. In an interview in 1986, before Kohl had even met the Soviet leader, Kohl compared Gorbachev to Nazi propaganda chief Joseph Goebbels. This insult not only demonstrated Kohl's distrust of the Soviet leader but also mortified Gorbachev and fueled his distrust of Kohl.

It wasn't the only barrier to trust between the two leaders. When Gorbachev was only 10 years old, he experienced the German invasion of his home village, Privolnoye, while his father was away in the military fighting the German invaders. Gorbachev watched the Germans leave his village in ruins and lived through the grief of thinking he had lost his father, who had been seriously wounded and was believed to be dead. Fortunately, his father survived the war.

Based on this history, Gorbachev had reasons to mistrust the Germans and their chancellor. But in order for Kohl to make his lifelong dream of Germany's reunification a reality, he needed Gorbachev as leader of the Soviet Union, which held control over East Germany, to agree to it. At first, collaboration on such a monumental agreement seemed out of reach. Yet less than four years later, Gorbachev agreed to the reunification of Germany. How these two men reached the point in their relationship that allowed for negotiating this agreement is a lesson in building trust that can be applied to building trust in leading businesses as well.

Before I share how they achieved this and how their lesson can be applied, let me offer a definition of trust.

What Is Trust?

The following definition of trust, which I paraphrase here, is from my colleague Charles Feltman:

Trust is the emotion that allows us to risk making something we value vulnerable to another person's actions.

Let's say you value your public reputation. Feeling trust toward a friend would make you feel comfortable to share information that could damage your reputation. In that sense, trusting your friend allows you to risk making your reputation vulnerable to your friend's actions. By trusting her, you are confident she wouldn't share it with anyone else. On the other hand, if you are not confident that your friend is committed and able to keep the information confidential, you wouldn't share it. This means that you distrust your friend to keep confidential the information that could damage your reputation.

Now let's explore what was at risk for Gorbachev that he valued and how he needed to assess whether he could take the risk of making it vulnerable to Kohl's actions. Gorbachev, as the leader of the Soviet Union, cared deeply about the future well-being of his country. The Soviet Union was struggling economically, and people were suffering because of that. Gorbachev was eager to reform the economy and needed economic help from Western countries, including the United States and West Germany. Kohl valued the reunification of his country and needed Gorbachev as the leader of the Soviet Union, which had control over East Germany, to agree to it. But Gorbachev's trauma of the German army ransacking his village when he was a child made it most important for him to protect his country and create the conditions for a lasting peace.

For that reason, after World War II, the Soviet Union and the Western allies had divided Germany into West and East to prevent it from ever posing a military threat to their countries again. For Gorbachev, a German reunification posed a possible risk to the post-war peace in Europe because he could not know what military ambitions a strengthened Germany would develop if he agreed to the reunification. For Kohl to get Gorbachev to agree to his lifelong dream, the reunification of Germany, he had to gain Gorbachev's trust, meaning he needed to help Gorbachev feel confident that a reunified Germany would not be a threat to the peace in Europe and to the Soviet Union.

To build trust, each of these leaders had to assess how the other was likely to act. Charles Feltman distinguishes four assessments to assess whether somebody can be trusted. These are *sincerity, reliability, competence and care.* They can be summarized this way:

Sincerity is the assessment that you say what you mean and mean what you say and act accordingly. It's about being honest with yourself and others. Gorbachev needed to be sure that Kohl was sincere about his and his country's commitment to peace and also to supporting the Soviet Union economically after a possible reunification.

Reliability is the assessment that others can count on you to deliver what you promise. It's about keeping commitments. Both men needed to trust that the other would be reliable to execute on their agreement.

Competence is the assessment that you have the ability to do what you are doing or propose to do. It's about having the requisite capacity, skill, knowledge, resources and time to do a particular task or job. Gorbachev and Kohl each needed to trust that the other man had the leadership competence to gain the needed support at home.

Care is the assessment that you have the other person's interest in mind as well as your own when you make decisions and take actions. It's fueled by empathy and is related to compassion and interest. Each of the two men had to get to know each other at a person-to-person level and to empathize with and care about the other.

Let's take a look at how they applied these four assessments to build trust.

Building Trust

To open the door for a meeting, Kohl first apologized for the Goebbels comparison. Because he had not yet been invited to meet with Gorbachev, he delivered his apology through Richard von Weizaecker, the president of West Germany, who visited Moscow in 1987.

This paved the way to the leaders' first meeting in October 1988 in Moscow. In the meeting, Kohl pointed out to Gorbachev that both were about the same age and that both of their families had lived through the horrors of the war. He also made reference to the fact that Gorbachev's father was wounded and that Kohl's own brother had died in the war at the age of 18, as described by

Gorbachev's biographer, William Taubman. Kohl empathized with the Soviet leader's childhood experience and demonstrated care about him as a human being. By sharing his own pain about losing his brother, Kohl helped Gorbachev to empathize with him in return.

This conversation may have also helped the Soviet leader assess the chancellor's sincerity about his commitment to peace because Gorbachev was touched by Kohl sharing his own childhood war trauma, witnesses of the exchange said. They proceeded to talk with each other not limited by their role as the leaders of their countries who represented opposing worldviews, but as two human beings. Gorbachev, who valued that personal connection, considered their first meeting a strategic turning point in Soviet-West German relations. A first step was made in building trust.

But more steps had to follow. Eight months later, in June 1989, Gorbachev visited Germany. During that visit, the two men met privately three times. At Kohl's home, where they had dinner with their wives, the two men shared stories about their childhoods and their families' suffering during the war. It was then that Kohl told Gorbachev that he liked his policy and liked him as a person. While these private meetings validated their assessments of each other's care and sincerity, by talking about their alignment on policies, they had also progressed to assessing each other's competence.

Gorbachev, during his visit in Bonn, said that he valued the trust that was growing between the two men at every meeting. One historian wrote that by the end of the visit, West Germany had become Moscow's "most important partner in Europe."

A year later, when Gorbachev received Kohl in Moscow in July of 1990, he took him on a tour of his home region, and they stayed overnight in a small VIP resort in the Caucasus Mountains, where they further deepened their relationship. The friendship that had grown between them was symbolized in an action of Gorbachev's wife, Raisa, who, upon their arrival at the resort where she had been picking flowers as she waited for them, presented the bouquet she had gathered to Kohl. In Russia, giving flowers to a person is a way of expressing warm feelings or gratitude for that person.

We cannot know for sure when, exactly, in the course of these meetings the two men recognized each other as a reliable partner. But by the time of the Caucasus meeting, they must have already reached that assessment. It was in this atmosphere of mutual trust that they sealed their deal on the reunification of Germany, which they announced the next day at a joint press conference.

While Gorbachev's agreement was greatly influenced by the political and economic crisis of the Soviet Union as well as by his greater vision of a unified Europe, without building trust, he might never have agreed to the reunification. Kohl, without learning to trust the Soviet leader, may not have been able to allow himself to make himself vulnerable and therefore give Gorbachev the opportunity to get to know and trust him at a deeper level.

You may wonder how this example of two world leaders building trust applies for you. *Sincerity, reliability, competence and care* are the four criteria that help all of us assess trust in any relationship. I use them to build trust in my personal relationships, and I have used them in my leadership roles and when I coach others to learn how to build trust.

Let me share the example of applying the four criteria of trust in my search for a software development partner after my project seemed suddenly derailed by my general manager's decision, as described in Chapter 4. When I learned that the internal software developers were not available anymore, I had to find an external software development partner I could trust to develop the product I had planned with my colleagues. I looked for a company that was willing to commit to investing upfront, had the right skill set and was passionate about the purpose of the project. In return, they would become a more strategic partner of a global company and receive a fair share in the financial success.

It was an attractive proposition for a smaller company that aspired to grow globally, but I wondered how I could make sure that I could trust the company that we would choose to be the right partner for our needs. I created a short list of candidates, which I evaluated using a list of criteria, such as their alignment with our goals and values and their competence and reliability. In the final round we had narrowed the list down to two companies, which I visited with a couple of my colleagues for a final review. As described earlier, trust has multiple dimensions. We asked questions that would help us assess how much they cared about our needs and those of our clients, their competence, sincerity and reliability.

During the visit with Company A, the formal reviews went very well. The engineers listened carefully to our needs, and we felt they had the competencies we were looking for. Yet I still had my doubts about the sincerity and reliability of their CEO. I was wondering what his real intentions were. As we came to the end of our visit on the second day, after long meetings, the CEO invited us for dinner, which gave me more opportunity to chat informally. I felt compelled to ask him, "Imagine we are wildly successful. What will you do?" Without pause, he replied, "Then I will find something I can make more money with!" In that moment, I had a strong feeling that his main motivation for signing the partnership agreement with us was to increase the valuation of his own company to sell it. We were looking for a long-term partnership, but now I sensed from his comments that as soon as he signed the contract he would try to sell his company, and we might end up with an unknown partner.

Then we did the same review with Company B. We spent two days in intense meetings, followed by more informal talks over dinner at night. Once again, I used the dinner visit to get to know the CEO of the second company on a more personal level. He shared with me how he had built his company from the ground up and how proud he was of that achievement. He talked about how his company provided the opportunity for people to have a career and that this partnership would allow his company to serve clients globally. This CEO had a true purpose. He wanted to build a great company that people were passionate about working for, serving clients worldwide. He also talked about the contribution he was making to the people in his country. I trusted his sincerity and integrity. I felt he was caring, while the CEO of Company A appeared driven by his own gain. On the last night of our visit, I felt comfortable in closing our deal and signing our partnership agreement. I never regretted that decision because the partnership became very successful.

Trust Is at the Heart of Leadership

Trust is at the heart of leadership because it affects every single one of the seven leadership behaviors and associated emotional drivers of the ASPIRE Leadership Model. Take a moment to put yourself into the shoes of your stakeholders, such as your employees, clients, investors or community. What questions might they ask to assess your care, sincerity, reliability and competence as the leader? Even if they don't express it openly, in the back of their mind, they ask:

Can I trust that you…

…*empathize* with and *care* about me as a human being? (care)

…are *compassionate* and committed to *serving* my needs? (care)

…are *interested* in and *understand* my needs and *understand* what it takes to meet them? (care, sincerity and competence)

…have a vision that is aligned with my aspirations, and your *optimism* about achieving it is authentic? (care and sincerity)

…are capable of *inspiring* and *mobilizing* the people and resources needed to make the vision a reality? (competence)

…are capable of *building* trust and *coordinating effective actions* toward the vision? (competence and reliability)

…will be *resilient* and *positive* in the face of adversity? (care, competence and reliability)

The first five questions are based on the behavioral and emotional competencies shared in Chapters 1–5. They create a strong foundation on which to build trust and foster collaboration. See the pyramid below.

ASPIRE Leadership Model © 2022 by Reiner Lomb

Let me point out that while trust builds on the previous five emotional competencies, trust also affects these emotions. For example, to be inspired by a leader and feel optimistic that a vision can become reality, a person needs to trust the leader.

Three Directions of Trust

For a leader, there are three directions of trust. One is people's trust in you as a leader, as described before. The second is your trust in the people you lead. The third is trust between the people you are leading. Following is a summary of all three directions of trust.

Trust in you as the leader: Developing trust with your stakeholders in you as a leader related to all seven emotional and behavioral competencies as described above is one direction of developing trust. This includes trusting yourself as the leader.

Trust by you in your stakeholders: The second direction in developing trust that is equally important for you as a leader is learning to trust others who follow and support your vision. This includes your employees, investors, clients or community.

Trust between your stakeholders: The third direction is the development of trust between all the stakeholders in order to foster effective collaboration. For example, if your team members trust you and you trust them, but they don't trust each other, they won't collaborate effectively.

All three directions of trust fuel the collaboration with and among the people you mobilize to make your vision a reality. The absence of trust in any of the three directions jeopardizes collaboration and, with that, the realization of your vision. Fortunately, research has shown that trust can be learned, and the practices later in this chapter can help you to develop trust in all three directions.

As with the other emotional competencies from previous chapters, understanding the barriers to trust can help you select practices that help you overcome them and develop trust. Before we go there, let me briefly share some additional benefits of building trust in organizations.

Other Benefits of Trust

From my own experience in working and coaching in organizations around the world, I observe that people want to work on teams and in organizations where trust is high, and they feel miserable if trust is low. Research has found that trust increases people's life satisfaction and the overall organizational performance. When trust is present, people suffer less chronic stress and are happier and healthier than people who work in companies where trust is low.

For countries, economists have found that a culture of trust is among the most powerful predictors to explain why some are prosperous while others are poor. Surveys conducted by Gallup have shown that two-thirds of adults worldwide believe corruption was widespread among businesses in their country, clearly a measure of low trust.

If the benefits are so compelling, what keeps leaders from developing trust? Following are some of the key barriers to building trust.

Barriers to Trust

Understanding the barriers to trust will help you in choosing the right practices for developing trust. One of the most overlooked barriers to trust is lack of self-trust. That's why I start with that.

Lack of Self-Trust

Just as self-compassion is a prerequisite to compassion for others, as explained in Chapter 2, self-trust is also a prerequisite, and its lack is a barrier to trusting others.

For example, when a person is faced with a challenge in life or at work that they can't see a solution for, I often ask:

"Do you trust that a solution exists, even if you can't see it right now?" If the person replies with, "Yes, I trust that a solution exists," the second question I ask is:

"Do you trust that with the right effort and support you will find that solution?"

In this way, trust in one's own ability extends to trust in others and vice-versa. This was shown to me when I was on a computer science research team with two other colleagues where none of us individually had the answers to the challenging questions we were chartered to research, but we trusted that answers existed and that we would find them with the right support from each other. This trust kept us inspired to collaborate. Self-trust fueled our trust in each other, and trust in each other fueled trust in ourselves. Seeing and experiencing the interrelationship between trust and self-trust was a eureka moment at a time in my young life where I still needed to develop self-trust. Looking back, that experience elevated my ability to collaborate to a whole new level.

Lack of Empathy, Compassion and Interest

Let's come back to the earlier definition of trust as *the emotion that allows us to risk making something we value vulnerable to another person's actions.* Would you risk sharing about your deepest needs and feelings with someone who you believe has no empathy and compassion or shows no interest in even listening to your needs? I would not and I assume you wouldn't either. Trust in another person builds on the person's empathy and compassion for and interest in your needs. Lack of empathy, compassion and interest by the other person is a barrier to trusting that person. Naturally, this applies to all three directions of trust.

Fear and Need for Invulnerability

While trust allows people to make something they value vulnerable to another person's actions, fear drives their need for invulnerability and is therefore a barrier to trust. This can be explained by the workings of our emotional threat and soothing systems described in Chapter 1. These systems have enabled us to survive and thrive throughout our human evolution. Our threat system, associated with a healthy level of fear and distrust, alerts us to threats and motivates us to take action such as protecting us from a potential aggressor. Fear that another person could harm us feeds our distrust and vice-versa. In today's work environment, our emotional threat system is often activated by perceived danger, such as from a colleague who we may see as a competitor when it comes to our career advancement. If that's the case, we won't risk making a possible promotion vulnerable to the actions of our colleague. I have observed that this learned competitive and protective behavior is hard to turn off for the benefit of a team.

On the other hand, if our emotional soothing system, associated with feeling safe, is activated, we are willing to risk making ourselves vulnerable to another person's actions. In that case, we see our colleague as a collaborator. Not feeling safe in such a relationship makes us want to be invulnerable and put our guard up. Fear and our need for invulnerability are interrelated.

Bias

Another barrier to trust is bias toward people from another group, such as another ethnicity, race, nationality, organization, function or role. Social science research has shown that people are willing to trust people of their own group more than people from another group. Bias is learned and it can be conscious and unconscious. Daryl Davis from Chapter 3 experienced conscious bias toward him from the Klan member because Daryl was Black. The Klan member believed that Black people were genetically predisposed to violence, and it made him fear and hate them. In that example, Daryl was able to bring the man's bias to the surface and help him overcome it. Unconscious bias means we are not aware of it, and because of that, it is much harder to overcome. This is, for example, the case when I see a person from another group and feel fear but cannot explain why I feel that way.

Dishonesty and Faking Competence

Sincerity is one of the four dimensions of trust, and it includes your assessment that the other person is honest. Dishonesty, even if observed only once, will become a barrier to trusting a leader's sincerity. In our time of online and social media, dishonesty, if exposed, can become visible in an instant to the whole world.

Typically, you are not going to ask your auto mechanic friend to cut your hair or your barber to repair your car. While you trust them in one area of competence, you won't trust them in the area in which they have no training or experience. This sounds like a simple assessment to make. Yet, when it comes to the domain of leadership, assessing one's leadership competence for a specific leadership situation is not so easy. In order to get the promotion or be selected for the leadership position, people tend to oversell their competencies or hide that they are lacking a competency. This is even true at the highest level in organizations. Research for the CEO Genome Project found that almost a quarter of CEOs who had been fired from their job had a lack of key skill-sets.

Breaking Promises or Making Ineffective Requests

Breaking promises without warning, and often with severe consequences for the ones to whom the promise was made, creates distrust in a person's reliability. For example, you committed to your manager to finish a time-critical project by Friday. Monday comes, and your manager still hasn't heard from you, and it affects a commitment that he has made to his manager. He is now totally caught off-guard because you had neglected to warn him that you wouldn't keep your commitment. In this example, the broken promise seems to be the fault of the person who made the commitment. Yet, often what looks like a broken promise in fact is the result of an ineffective request.

An ineffective request happens when you ask someone without verifying whether he is ready to receive the request or able to understand it. I have seen this happen when someone shouts out a request to a colleague who has something else on his mind, such as hurrying to another appointment. Your colleague in passing mumbles something and nods. You believe he understands your request and is committed to fulfill it. However, that may not be the case, and it is your responsibility to make sure that your request is heard, understood and to confirm the commitment.

Both cases, breaking promises and ineffective requests, often lead to the request not being fulfilled, and that leads to distrusting the person who the request was made to even if it was the fault of the person who made the request. If unattended, this leads to distrust in return.

The Cycle of High Level of Stress and Distrust

Research by Paul J. Zak has shown that when we feel trusted by others our brain produces the brain chemical oxytocin. In return, increased oxytocin makes us trust the other person. In other words, our brains reward us for trusting each other and for collaborating. While oxytocin makes us feel good to be part of a team or an organization, high levels of stress, such as those caused by distrust, inhibits the release of oxytocin and has proven to be a barrier to trust.

Maybe you have experienced one or more of the previous barriers to trust. Before you read on, I encourage you to think about what challenges around trust you have experienced or may be experiencing right now. Think of a person you or others on your team have a challenging relationship with and with whom lack of trust prevents effective collaboration. Ask yourself which of the previous barriers may be causing this.

Keep those barriers in mind as you read through the following best practices for building trust.

Developing Trust: Best Practices

Let's look at best practices for developing trust in each of the three directions of trust: Trust in you as a leader, by you in others and between your stakeholders.

Develop Trust in You as a Leader

Trust in you as a leader is affected by the assessments your stakeholders, such as your employees, clients, investors or community, make in regard to your care, sincerity, reliability and competence. Practicing the seven emotional and behavioral competencies of the ASPIRE Leadership Model in a consistent way will lead to a positive assessment in these four dimensions of trust.

Your practice of caring, understanding and serving, which build the foundation of the ASPIRE leadership pyramid, as described in Chapters 1–3, will allow your stakeholders to assess you as caring and sincere. As mentioned previously, when I worked at Hewlett-Packard, I learned a practice that the founders, Dave and Bill, had modeled called "management by walking around." It was a common practice by HP managers around the world to wander around in an unstructured manner through offices and manufacturing floors and randomly check with employees on the status of their ongoing work. It allowed the managers to demonstrate their interest in their teams, help them empathize with and understand their needs and, if needed, provide the right support. I observed that this common practice helped to foster trust in management. In fact, trust in management during those years was very high at HP.

This may sound great for people who work at the same location, but what if teams are regionally distributed? While you find it a lot easier to build trust when you are in the same location with your stakeholders, you can also apply these practices to environments where they are remote. For most of my career, I had teams located around the world. I would virtually "wander around" by following the sun around the globe.

These brief and frequent check-ins are not only essential for building trust but also for maintaining it because our understanding of a conversation we had with another person may diverge over time. When we are in the same office, we have more opportunities to talk and converge again. That's why in remote situations I recommend establishing the practice of brief and frequent virtual check-ins with your stakeholders, even if you believe there's no issue.

Once you have laid a foundation of trust by practicing caring, serving and understanding, the next level is to practice visioning, mobilizing, coordinating effective actions and resilience. Demonstrating these leadership behaviors will allow your stakeholders to assess questions they ask themselves about your competence as a leader, such as, "Can I trust that your vision is really aligned with my needs?" "Can I trust that you will be able to mobilize the resources needed to bring this vision to fruition?" "Will you be able to coordinate effective actions?" and, "Will you be resilient when challenges occur?" It will be your consistency in practicing the seven leadership behaviors that build trust in you as a leader.

Note that the seventh behavior, resilience, will be covered in Chapter 7 in more detail.

Learn to Trust Others

Equally important to your stakeholders' trust in you is your trust in them. Justified distrust may help you protect what you value from someone's careless, incompetent or even ill-intended actions. In that case, distrust serves an important purpose. Unjustified distrust, on the other hand, can keep you from engaging people that are committed to support your vision. For example, if members on your team feel distrusted by you, despite their trustworthiness, they will feel resentment and distrust toward you in return. It can become a reinforcing loop of distrust that prevents effective collaboration between your stakeholders and you.

You can overcome distrust by learning to trust. When Kohl made the negative public comment about Gorbachev, the chancellor demonstrated his distrust in the new Soviet leader before he even gave it a chance to get to know him. With that, he jeopardized making his lifelong dream of the German reunification a reality. Gorbachev resented Kohl for his distrustful remarks and would not meet with him until after Kohl had apologized.

Learning to trust others can be challenging, particularly someone you are just getting to know or someone you have known and trusted but who has done something that makes you question your trust in that person. In both situations, learning to trust someone new or to rebuild trust, engaging in dialogue and taking the risk to openly talk about the areas of concern is a critical step. When preparing for these conversations, it's important to ask yourself,

"In which of the four dimensions of trust—sincerity, reliability, competence and care—do I question the trustworthiness of the other person?"

If it's someone new, such as hiring or negotiating a new business partnership, you may want to assess all four dimensions. Before assessing the person, be clear about what your expectations are in terms of sincerity, reliability, competence and care. For example, if you are a school principal hiring a new teacher, you may want to find someone who truly cares about the students, is sincere about it, has shown that he is competent to teach the required subject and is reliable, such as showing up on time. Be as specific as possible about your expectations in all four dimensions of trust so it will be clear for you what to look for when you engage with the person. At the end, your hiring decision will be based on the trust you have gained in the candidate during the hiring process.

If a situation involves someone you have trusted, but a recent experience makes you question the person's trustworthiness, you may be able to identify just one or two of the four dimensions of trust. Let's say one of your team members used to finish projects on time but in recent weeks has missed several deadlines. In this situation, questioning all four dimensions of trust may not be helpful. Instead, it will be more effective to focus your conversation with the employee on the issue of reliability and the actions needed to rebuild trust in that dimension.

In the end, learning and developing trust in others is not a one-time exercise. It's an ongoing effort, and knowing what dimension of trust is in question allows you to take more targeted action, the way that Kohl and Gorbachev did. Each of them cared deeply about a peaceful coexistence of their countries and therefore assessed each other on their sincerity in that dimension of trust. These men succeeded in that, even if their successors still struggle in that area today.

Facilitate Trust Between Your Stakeholders

I suggest two ways to facilitate building trust between your team members or other stakeholders:

The first is *creating opportunities for team members to get to know each other on a personal level.* I learned to appreciate this approach to trust-building when I took my global teams on offsite meetings where I created opportunities for team members to get to know each other personally through joint activities. Taking people out of the high-stress work environment into a more playful setting helps to remove stress as a barrier to trust and collaboration.

The second one, which I learned from my colleague, Phil Sandhal, is *engaging people in a disagreement successfully and surviving it by focusing on the issues and not the person.* As the leader of a team, you can proactively facilitate the process of engaging in and surviving a conflict by setting the rules for the conversation and holding everybody accountable to follow these rules. For example, give each person an equal opportunity to share their perspective, remind others to listen, and then allow each person to give feedback in a way that focuses on the issue and not the person.

Doing this will not only increase the trust between your team members but also increase the trust by the team in you as a leader and help you grow self-trust in your ability to lead your team through conflicts in the future. Investing time in facilitating trust-building between your team members will help you build a high-performing team for the long run.

Let's summarize the key insights about trust as a fuel for collaboration.

Summary:

- ✓ Once you mobilize people to support your vision, you must coordinate effective actions to bring it to fruition. This requires collaboration with and among the people you have mobilized.

- ✓ Trust is the emotion that enables people to collaborate. Lack of trust hinders collaboration.

- ✓ That's why trust is the sixth of the seven essential emotions for leading change, and research shows that high-trust organizations perform better and have healthier, happier and more engaged employees.

- ✓ Trust can be defined as the emotion that allows us to make something we value vulnerable to another person's actions. Inviting others to collaborate in the pursuit of the vision you value makes it vulnerable to their actions.

✓ To assess if somebody can be trusted, we distinguish four assessments: *sincerity, reliability, competence and care.*

✓ When you assess trust in your organization, there are three directions of trust you need to pay attention to: trust in you as the leader, trust between your stakeholders and your trust in your stakeholders.

✓ Trust builds on the seven essential leadership emotions and behaviors, including trust and collaboration itself, and it can be learned and developed.

✓ To develop trust, first assess which of the three directions of trust and then which of the four aspects of trust (care, sincerity, competence and reliability) need development. Then choose the right practice(s).

Pause and Reflect

Before you continue reading, I recommend pausing a moment and reflecting:

• Who are my most critical stakeholders?
• How much trust do they feel for me, for each other, and how much trust do I feel for them?

Trust:

1...2...3...4...5...6...7...8...9...10

If trust is lower than eight in any of three directions, ask yourself, "What are the biggest barriers to trust, and what can I practice to develop that direction of trust?"

Now that we have addressed the importance for a leader to foster collaboration, and trust as the fuel for collaboration, the next chapter will explore the importance of resilience in the face of obstacles and how positivity builds resilience.

"Do not judge me by my success;
judge me by how many times I fell down and got back up again."
~ Nelson Mandela

CHAPTER 7:

Positivity – Being Resilient

The emotional competencies of Chapters 1–3—empathy, compassion and interest—help you with caring about, committing to serving and understanding people's needs and issues better. These first three competencies lay the foundation for the next three emotional competencies of Chapters 4–6—optimism, inspiration and trust. Optimism helps you envision a future in which the needs of the people you care about are fully met and the issues related to meeting those needs are resolved. Inspiration helps you to mobilize people, and trust helps you to coordinate effective actions to make your vision a reality.

Once you have embarked on your journey to make your vision reality, even the best planning may not prepare you for all the adversities that can get in the way of reaching your goals. That's why the final of the seven essential behavioral competencies is resilience.

Resilience is the ability to recover from setbacks, overcome roadblocks, adapt well to change and keep going in the face of adversity.

Developing resilience is a lifelong pursuit because life's demands on us change constantly, often without any warning or time to prepare. When I started writing this chapter, for example, COVID-19 appeared like a few distant clouds on the horizon, but by the time I reached the end, it had paralyzed cities and countries around the world. Fear about the growing numbers of infections and deaths shut down public life, collapsing the economy, with millions losing their livelihood. Growing anxiety caused panic sell-offs in the stock market along with hoarding of goods.

Not immune to the general mood, my family and I, like others, were rushing to the store to make sure we had enough supplies for a weeks-long shutdown. As I write these words, we have been confined at home for nearly a month with no end date in sight. Helping to homeschool our daughter while trying to work at the same time caused me to abandon my old routine that used to keep me emotionally, mentally and physically balanced. The changes also brought a big setback on my journey to complete the book. As I struggled with many new challenges in my day and roadblocks in my routine, I was also supporting my wife and daughter with the shifts happening in their lives and that of our family. In addition, I was striving in my work to be there for my clients during their crises and adversity. There were many ways in which I needed to adapt, on many fronts, and one of them was to postpone my original publishing date and plans.

This experience gave me a renewed perspective about how these behaviors—recovering from setbacks, overcoming roadblocks, adapting to change and continuing on in the face of adversity— are all part of being resilient. I was also reminded of what type of emotions support resilience and what type may destroy it. Let's start with the latter ones.

Negativity Destroys Resilience

Negative emotions destroy resilience. Initially, when the pandemic began, I had failed to shield myself from the negativity in the media or in communication with others. After a week at home, I was at risk of spiraling into a negative mood and infecting my family with it. For me, as for billions of people around the world, the pandemic was a sudden setback that brought a reversal of progress in many areas of my life. Whether it was my new role of overseeing our daughter's schooling, worries about family members far away or the existential crisis some of my clients faced, I saw that if I slipped into a negative mood, it jeopardized my ability to be resilient.

In those early days, I hadn't adapted well to the change the pandemic meant for my life and, more so, for my work. In fact, I felt resentment toward certain people because of what I thought was careless behavior toward others. I felt anxiety because of the uncertainty about the future and fear for the safety of my loved ones and myself. After I received feedback from my wife about my negative mood, I realized that I had to stop the downward spiral of negativity, not just for me but for others too. Many of my experiences, including the following example, have taught me that one very important role of a leader is to shift away from negativity for the sake of everyone's well-being and resilience, whether in the family, the community or the workplace.

On one beautiful October day in the Colorado Rocky Mountains years ago, I had gathered my newly formed global work team at a hotel for a three-day retreat. We were there to plan and coordinate our business development activities around the world for the next year. Our business had been on a fast-track pace of growth in a new and competitive market. To keep that momentum, I'd been able to mobilize additional resources and recruit a new team of people from around the world. Since it was the start of a new fiscal year, it was time to prioritize and coordinate our actions for the next 12 months. This was a highly talented group of people, yet still a newly assembled team. To succeed, the group had to learn to collaborate effectively as a team despite being located in different locations around the world.

That's why I was excited about having the whole team gathered in the same location for three days of face-to-face meetings. To give people the opportunity to get to know each other better at a personal level, I'd also planned some fun activities, such as hiking in the nearby mountains. My intention was to create a positive, joyful atmosphere where people would thrive creatively and engage in constructive dialogue.

On the morning of the first day, the meeting started on a positive note. The conference room had big windows with a view of the mountains illuminated by the rising sun. We began with introductions and then launched into the topics of discussion. Everything seemed to go well, but after lunch, coinciding with dark clouds that covered the peaks of the Rockies, I noticed a dark mood starting to overshadow our meeting. I sensed tension rising slowly between two team members sitting across the table from each other.

One had been working in this business for a couple of years, and the other was new to it. From different countries, they were meeting for the first time. Both were highly accomplished professionals and had the same role and responsibility in their geographic region.

Whenever we discussed a topic and one of them shared his view, the other would attack immediately and vice-versa. This started subtly but soon increased in intensity. At some point, the attacks became personal and had nothing to do with the topic. Threat-focused emotions such as fear and anger seemed to trap them in an automatic cycle of reacting to each other's attacks, hijacking their rational mind. As the other team members watched, the verbal attacks between these two affected the mood of the whole team. I could see in people's facial expressions that they were becoming frustrated, and I noticed that they were disengaging from the conversation.

If the behavior of these two continued, I felt that the meeting would be a failure, and the animosity would linger and hinder effective collaboration going forward. What had started as a beautiful morning full of possibilities had, by afternoon, been overshadowed by their actions and the negative mood it had created for the team. I knew intuitively then what research has now confirmed, that negativity always weakens our ability to be resilient. This means that the team would not have the ability to recover from that emotional setback and would stay in a negative mood throughout the duration of the meeting.

Whether we spread negativity or positivity is a choice. In the heat of their arguments, the two team members had been unaware, as they later admitted, that their negativity toward each other had brought the mood of the whole team down. One negative comment can ignite an endless cycle of negative responses and spiral out of control, as we can observe in all parts of our society, most visibly on social media. Such negativity directed toward one person or group affects the mood of everyone who is observing. For example, how you talk about your competitors will be noticed by your clients, employees and partners. How you talk about a leader from another team (department, business, etc.) has an effect on the people on your team, as does how you as a parent talk about the neighbor in front of your children. All of these actions affect others' emotional state.

The dynamic that developed with my team that day caught me by surprise. I didn't understand the cause of the conflict, so I called for a break to create some space. I wanted to stop the downward spiral and also understand what was going on between the two team members.

To clarify, I am not encouraging that you discount or suppress negative emotions. In fact, negative emotions are valuable because they connect us to the vast capacity of our subconscious mind, such as its ability to sense danger long before our conscious mind can or alerting us that important boundaries have been violated and we must pay attention and understand what is wrong. Numbing or blocking negative emotions prevents us from learning—and from growing to become more resilient. Yet as this example shows, there are many situations in which even the slightest bit of negativity can spiral out of control and spread to others very rapidly, like a cancer, if left unaddressed.

To interrupt the downward spiral of negativity, I had to understand what caused their negative emotions, so I interrupted the meeting for a coffee break. During the break, I asked the two team members to join me for a walk. There, out in nature, with a calm voice, I shared how I and the other team members were experiencing their attacks on each other and how that created a negative mood for the whole team. Sharing my observations had an effect on them. I had been afraid they would become defensive, but to my surprise, and to their credit, they opened up and I learned from them that what had happened in the meeting was that each of them felt threatened by the other in their position on the team. As a reaction to that perceived threat, they had slipped into a fight response. I made it clear that to achieve our ambitious goals, the whole team needed them to collaborate. Both apologized, and it sounded sincere. When we rejoined the rest of the team, they also apologized to the team, and for the remainder of the meeting they actually set an example for creating a positive mood in the group.

In Chapter 6, I had shared that one of the practices for building trust is to *engage people in a disagreement successfully and survive it by focusing on the issues and not the person.* As the leader of a team, you can proactively facilitate the process of engaging in and surviving a conflict by setting the rules for the conversation and holding everybody accountable to follow these rules. For example, by giving each person an equal opportunity to share their perspective and ensuring that others are listening and then allowing each person to give feedback in a way that focuses on the issue and not the person. That's what I had done on my walk with the two team members.

My approach with them was to help them become aware of their negative emotions (fear and anger), understand what thoughts (or story) were associated with them ("He is a competitor") and help them change the story ("He is a partner"). This allowed their emotions to shift. In hindsight, I was grateful that the conflict within this newly formed team had become visible so early so that we could fail quickly, learn from it and create a sustainable emotional shift. In this incident, negative emotions were not suppressed but used as a window into underlying issues that we were then able to resolve and shift the team into a positive mood. Positivity helps us to become more resilient, and in that way we used this crisis to become more resilient as a team.

Now let's look at how positivity builds resilience and what it means.

Positivity Builds Resilience

As illustrated in this previous example, research conducted by Barbara Frederickson now confirms that positive emotions have both a physical and mental effect on resilience. Resilient people use positivity as a "reset" button, Frederickson suggests. While their heart rate and blood pressure spike as much as those of people who are less resilient, when put into a stressful situation, their heart rate and blood pressure come down faster when they don't allow themselves to spiral into negativity. They also rebound faster emotionally.

If you struggle with bouncing back from sudden setbacks or adversities, you can build your resilience by increasing your amount of positivity relative to your amount of negativity, which is called the positivity-to-negativity ratio. According to Frederickson's research, feeling three or more positive emotions for every negative emotion promotes resilience. In other research, John Gottman studied the interactions between couples, and he found that the ratio of five positive interactions or higher to one negative interaction is a favorable predictor of a happy and stable marriage. Interestingly, applying Gottman's five-to-one ratio to relationships at work has also been proven to help create more effective teams.

Frederickson's three-to-one ratio of positive to negative emotions serves as a tipping point, which will help you determine whether you are resilient to life's setbacks or adversities. In my own experience, I aim for the five-to-one ratio or higher to be on the safe side. You can increase your positivity-to-negativity ratio by decreasing your amount of negativity and/or increasing your positivity. I want to re-emphasize that I don't suggest positivity at all costs or so-called toxic positivity, but rather to deal with negative emotions and specifically their sources in a healthy and productive way.

Going back to my own example of the early days of COVID-19, through my wife's feedback, I had realized that my grumpiness had affected the mood of our family and was jeopardizing our ability to be resilient. That's when I recognized that I needed to avoid being affected by the gloomy tone in the news, which was one major reason for my negative mood. Instead, I wanted to identify sources I could connect to that would allow me to experience more often positive emotions such as joy or humor. Let's take a deeper look at what positivity is.

Positivity – A Palette of Emotions

Unlike the previous six essential emotions for leading positive change in the ASPIRE Leadership Model, positivity, the emotional driver of resilience, consists of a palette of emotions. These include the previous six emotions—*empathy, compassion, interest, optimism, inspiration and trust*—and others, such as *aspiration, amusement, awe, enthusiasm, gratitude, hope, joy, peace, love and pride.* Let's see how the first six emotions may affect resilience and then explore the others.

In the previous example, when I allowed the continuous flow of negative news about COVID-19 to affect my own mood, my wife showed empathy with, compassion for and interest in my feelings about the situation. She did this by listening to my concerns, empathizing with my feelings and offering support. But she also shared how my negativity affected her mood and therefore helped me see that I jeopardized the resilience of my family during this crisis. I listened, and out of compassion and love for my family I made a commitment to help elevate our mood—in other words, to look for ways to feel and act more positively. Mutual empathy, compassion and interest had a positive effect on our relationship at that critical time. Note that simply taking interest in the other person's concerns already creates a positive shift. And it naturally builds trust in ourselves and in each other because we learn that we can count on each other for support in challenging times. Once I realized this, I felt inspired to use the pandemic as an opportunity to learn and grow my ability to be resilient.

In a similar way, I had used empathy, compassion and interest during the conflict between the two teammates I described earlier, and it increased the team's trust that we could overcome conflict and collaborate effectively. This emotional shift paved the way for feeling optimistic about the team's future.

In addition to the previous six emotions that can help you be more resilient, other common emotions that can help build resilience include aspiration, amusement, awe, enthusiasm, gratitude, hope, joy, peace, love and pride. Let's look at each in more detail.

Aspiration is associated with being drawn to grow or seek something higher, such as the need for self-actualization or an even higher purpose as discussed in Chapter 4. Feeling aspiration in that way is what makes you want to lead and create change in the first place. Aspiration is what kept me motivated to continue writing this book when setbacks happened and adversities showed up. Aspiration made me more resilient.

Amusement is the emotion you feel when something unexpected happens that makes you laugh or smile. As a leader, sharing something that makes people laugh or smile can launch a meeting in a more light-hearted atmosphere. In such an atmosphere, people collaborate better and are more creative. Sometimes I recognize the irony of an adversity, and it makes me smile about it. This moment of amusement prevents me from sliding into negativity and allows me to better cope with that situation.

Awe is the emotion you feel when something makes you stop in your tracks and you feel part of something larger than yourself. That is why awe is regarded as one of the transcendent emotions. Feeling awe is like being in a magic moment. For me, moments of awe may occur when I watch a beautiful sunset, listen to the power of the ocean waves or see the beauty of an eagle gliding in the sky.

Enthusiasm is associated with being committed to a noble or divine cause. Chapter 5, about inspiration, gave examples of leaders who inspire people through their enthusiasm, like Juergen Klopp, the Liverpool team manager enthusiastically firing up his team from the sideline.

Gratitude is the emotion we feel when we appreciate with all our heart something that has come our way as a gift to be treasured. This could be a friendship, our health, the work we have or even a challenge in life we are grateful for because it allows us to grow. Feeling gratitude is appreciating that the glass is half full instead of being disappointed that it is half empty.

Hope is the emotion we feel when things are dire, but we believe that they can change for the better. This is the emotion I recommend you cultivate when you cannot see how things can get better. You may say to yourself, "I don't know how I can overcome my challenge or how my situation is going to improve, but if I give it enough time or find the right help, things may get better, or I may figure it out."

Joy is when we feel life is good and we want to celebrate it. It sparks good vibrations in our body. Some define joy as an attitude and happiness as a destination because happiness carries an expectation of some external condition to be fulfilled or something to be achieved, while joy carries no expectation. For example, if you have failed to achieve an important goal, you may feel unhappy, but you can still feel joy by paying attention to the things in life that are sources of joy for you.

Peace is the feeling that all is well, and we rest without worry. It's the feeling we may aspire to when we are fighting doubt, fear or anxiety so that we'll be able to rest. When we are in a conflicted relationship, we may declare peace to one another, or if we are conflicted within ourselves, we may declare the desire for peace. Setting this tone and intention can help us shift from negativity. Mindfulness practices can help to feel peace.

Love is associated with a feeling of connectedness and even oneness with another person. In that sense, love is a transcendent emotion because it makes us feel part of the greater humanity. Often, we use the word "love" when we like the pleasant or good characteristics of a person. But love is not limited to that. Part of love is accepting and cherishing the other person in their entirety, including their negative characteristics. Think about a parent who, independent of some negative behaviors of the child, still loves the child wholeheartedly. The same might apply for the love of a child for its parents. A child might dislike certain characteristics or behaviors of a parent but still love the parent.

Love encompasses other positive emotions. For example, love is related to empathy and compassion, where we resonate emotionally with the person we love, and we want nothing more than for that person to be well and thrive. When we feel love for someone, we also feel gratitude about this person being in our life and joy when we are with that person.

Pride is the feeling of having done a good job and the desire to tell others about it. You may remember an achievement you have felt proud about, such as graduating from school, creating something important to you, winning a competition or something else you did well. Research shows that when we feel pride, we are more likely to persist when a task becomes difficult. While pride is clearly a positive emotion, one can take it too far and boast or brag about their achievements. That's why pride needs to be balanced with humility.

Serenity is a mindful state when all is well and we have the urge to savor our current circumstances. It is similar to feeling peace, and we will likely have the desire to find ways to integrate the serene experience into our lives more fully and more often. I felt such serenity on a recent trip to the mountains when I was sitting on the patio of a cabin overlooking the lush green of a forest that reached all the way to the horizon. I felt all was well, safe and comfortable, and I soaked it in. I had the desire to savor it, and when we left, I told my family, "We have to do this more often!"

The previous list of emotions is offered as a menu of options to help you develop positivity and build resilience. You certainly don't have to practice all of these emotions to support your resilience. I suggest practicing the ones that call to you in particular moments. In the end, what counts is your ratio of the amount of positive emotions relative to the amount of negative emotions you feel. Feeling five times more positive than negative will help you be more resilient.

Positivity and resilience complete the ASPIRE Leadership Model. See below. Developing empathy (care), compassion (serving), interest (understanding), optimism (vision), inspiration (mobilization) and trust (collaboration) will result in a strong foundation on which to develop positivity and build resilience.

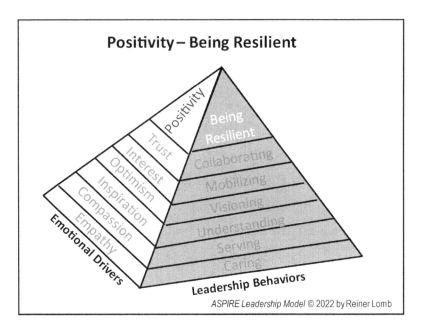

ASPIRE Leadership Model © 2022 by Reiner Lomb

Before we move into practices that help with increasing your positivity relative to your negativity, let's examine some of the typical barriers to positivity—and therefore to resilience.

Barriers to Positivity

As you read through the following list of barriers to positivity, I recommend taking note of any of the barriers you recognize as your own so you can keep those in mind when you choose your practice(s) for increasing your positivity relative to your negativity.

Negative Thinking and Rumination

Negative thinking breeds negative emotions such as anxiety, fear, anger, resentment, shame, guilt or contempt. Fear and anger drove the verbal attacks of the two team members at my retreat. Each thought of the other as a threat to his own position on the team, and it created fear and anger. Resentment is the emotion associated with the feeling of victimhood and contempt is the emotion associated with feeling that nothing good can come from the other person. They each feed a cycle of negative thoughts about others.

Shame and guilt, on the other hand, feed the negative cycle of thoughts about ourselves. We feel guilt when we have violated our own values or standards, such as not keeping a promise. It may make us feel less than other people, or we may even want to punish ourselves. While guilt is a private emotion, shame, on the other hand, is the assessment that we have broken the standards of our community, and it may lead to trying to hide from judgment and punishment. Both guilt and shame cloud your vision, and it makes it hard to see possibilities for overcoming challenging situations.

Rumination is when your mind goes over and over something bad that has happened, such as an argument with someone. This feeds an endless cycle of negative emotions and negative thinking that gets you stuck, and you quickly become overwhelmed and demoralized. Ruminating doesn't allow you to think clearly, and it multiplies negative emotions.

Suppressing negative thoughts and emotions: One approach many people take to overcome negative thoughts and emotions is to suppress them, such as by avoiding expressing them or pretending everything is fine, which is called toxic positivity. But science shows that the attempt to suppress negative thoughts and emotions can actually increase the misery. In fact, the numbing of the negative emotions robs us of the opportunity to learn, which keeps us from becoming more resilient.

Difficult Relationships

Managing difficult relationships and politics in the workplace was highlighted as the biggest drain on resilience at work in a British workplace survey. As the previous example of the team conflict demonstrates, it triggers threat-focused emotions such as anxiety, fear and anger. While these emotions have been important for our survival throughout our evolution, they can become a huge barrier to resilience in managing difficult relationships at work because they hijack our prefrontal cortex in moments of setbacks, when what we most need is to find creative solutions to overcome them.

Critical Feedback

Critical feedback threatens two of our most fundamental psychological needs: safety and self-worth. Joseph Grenny, who studied the effect of criticism on resilience, found that people who received harsh criticism experienced a whole range of negative emotions. A large majority described feeling dumbfounded, flabbergasted, shocked, stunned or numb. Others described a shame-related emotion like feeling embarrassed, worthless, hurt, sad and experiencing self-doubt. Some reported feelings that focused on the other person, such as anger and betrayal. All of these negative emotions impair our ability to be resilient because they decrease our positivity ratio.

Exhaustion and Burnout

Overwork and exhaustion are the opposite of resilience. This was confirmed in the previously mentioned survey, in which employees emphasized that the volume or pace of work stretched them to their limits. It was the second biggest drain on resilience. If this happens constantly, it may lead to burnout, which is recognized as a depressive condition. I have heard people who feel burned out say, "I can't go on anymore," and, "I have nothing left to give." Burnout is a huge barrier to resilience. If you suffer from burnout, I urge you to ask for professional help.

Despair

Despair is the emotion we feel when a situation seems unbearable and we don't have any hope that it will get better. This is the situation Viktor E. Frankl described when he observed fellow concentration camp inmates trading their last piece of bread for a cigarette, which he himself had contemplated in a moment of great despair when he was anticipating another encounter with a cruel SS Guard.

The previous barriers to positivity, and therefore resilience, are some of the typical barriers I have observed. I encourage you to reflect on your own barriers using the previous examples as a starting point, but also be open to others that might keep you from being resilient.

As you have seen throughout the examples in the previous chapters, as the leader you can greatly affect the emotions and moods of the people you lead. For example, Jennifer from Chapter 1, in order to motivate her team, threatened them and as a result created resentment and distrust, negative emotions that reduce the ability of the team to be resilient. Traci's actions, on the other hand, aimed to inspire. This encouraging approach contributed to her team's resilience. In the same way, you have the choice to cultivate other positive emotions, such as aspiration, amusement, awe, joy or pride that not only boost your own resilience but also the resilience of your team, organization or community.

Following are some best practices for increasing your positivity ratio, the amount of positivity related to the amount of negativity. As you read through them, keep in mind which of the barriers you are trying to overcome in order to increase your positivity and/or decrease your negativity.

Increasing Your Positivity and Decreasing Negativity: Best Practices

Increasing your positivity ratio will make you more resilient, and it can be achieved by decreasing your negativity or increasing positivity or both. This can sometimes feel hard to measure. As a straightforward approach I'd like to offer you the simple "How was my day?" exercise that you can do at the end of a day.

"How Was My Day?" Exercise

The "How was my day?" exercise starts with reflecting on your experiences during the course of the day from when you get up in the morning until the evening. Count the number of positive and negative interactions and reactions that you experience, and divide the number of positive by the number of negative ones. The result provides an estimate of your positivity ratio for that day. You can then repeat this exercise for a week to get a more balanced measure because emotions change. If you find your positivity ratio too low (less than five), find yourself being too negative or others signaling to you that you are too negative, you may try one or more of the following practices.

Each of these practices is designed to allow you to connect to a source or multiple sources that may increase your positivity or reduce your negativity. From these sources, we can feed our emotions, as the following story, a Cherokee Metaphor suggests.

Cherokee Metaphor

One evening an old Cherokee told his grandson
about a battle that goes on inside people.

He said, "My son, the battle is between
two wolves inside us all.

"One is Evil.
It is anger, envy, jealousy, sorrow, regret, greed,
arrogance, self-pity, guilt, resentment, inferiority, lies,
false pride, superiority and ego.

"The other is Good.
It is joy, peace, love, hope, serenity, humility, kindness,
benevolence, empathy, generosity, truth, compassion and faith."

The grandson thought about this for a minute
and then asked his grandfather:
"Which wolf wins?"

The old Cherokee simply replied,
"The one you feed."

As you read through the following best practices, open yourself up to your own ideas for connecting to these sources from which you feed the good within you. You may even identify your own best sources by asking, "What can I connect to that will disrupt my negative thoughts and emotions and create positive feelings such as aspiration, amusement, awe, enthusiasm, inspiration, interest, gratefulness, hope, joy and more?"

Connecting to a Higher Purpose

A higher purpose is a cause that is aligned with your highest values, a cause you deeply care and are absolutely passionate about. For example, I care deeply about the future of our children and children's children, and that's why I aspire to help create a future in which the way we live is more sustainable. That is also why in the middle of my corporate career I went back to university to study sustainability. I came out of that experience with the understanding that the issues we are facing are so huge that it requires millions and millions of people around the world to be mobilized and empowered to help create change. As a result of my studies, I decided to focus my work on mobilizing and developing leaders who aspire to create a better future.

Chapter 4 explains how to create such an aspirational vision. Having a higher purpose and a vision that is aligned with that purpose inspires and therefore generates a deep and sustained commitment to act. I have observed the same with many of my clients. People who have a strong purpose are more resilient, a truth also supported by research. The same is true for a team or an organization. Having a common purpose helps the whole team or organization be more resilient.

Viktor E. Frankl's experience in the concentration camps led him to observe how easily he and his companions could give up or succumb to despair. Yet, he didn't give up but was inspired to endure, determined to survive and to write and publish about his experiences in the camps. This became his book, *Man's Search for Meaning*. Writing down and sharing his observations with the world was his purpose and reason to survive. His book has inspired millions to find hope and resilience, purpose and meaning

Connecting to Self

The greatest source of positivity is within us. This means that by learning to manage our thoughts, beliefs and emotions, we can build resilience. There are many ways to connect to ourselves as a source of positivity and to reduce negativity. Following are several practices that I find useful. They include becoming more mindful, accepting and facing reality, disputing negative thinking, breaking the grip of rumination, dealing with negative people, creating a recovery period, such as exercising, using a powerful mantra and creating distance.

Become more mindful: Research has shown that a regular mindfulness practice like meditation reduces activity in the brain circuits linked with negativity and increases activity in our brain circuits that are linked with positivity. Other examples of mindfulness practices may include a walk in nature, listening to music or conscious breathing. It sounds counterintuitive to step back in a moment of sudden adversity because we may have the desire to lean in and tackle the challenge we are facing. But in that moment, negative thoughts and associated emotions such as anger, fear or anxiety may prevent us from seeing the best way forward. In such situations, a good night's sleep, a period of meditation or a walk in the woods have often helped me shift my mood to such positive emotions as gratitude, joy, peace, hope—even optimism. In those emotional states, I could see more possibilities to act and overcome my adversities.

Accept and face reality: Facing the reality of the bad thing that happened to us and accepting it is an important emotional shift that helps us move forward. From acceptance, we can shift to hope or reality-grounded optimism, as discussed in Chapter 4. The faster you can shift to acceptance, the more resilient you will be because you will spend less time and energy on denial or on fighting what you cannot change. Acceptance is the emotion from which it will be easier to shift to hope and optimism, which give you a lens into future possibilities. The acceptance I suggest here does not mean you have to like or approve of what happened; it is about not fighting what you cannot change.

Dispute negative thinking: Negative thinking can become a cycle in which the negative thoughts feed negative emotions, which then feed the negative thinking. While this is an energy-draining cycle that is hard to stop, and also a complex topic to deal with, you can break the cycle by disputing the negative thinking that triggers the cycle in the first place. Start with trying to observe your negative thoughts objectively. When you identify a recurring negative thought such as, "My boss is planning to fire me," ask yourself, "Is the source of my thought external or internal?" You might also answer by asking, "Do I assume this, or do I know this for sure, and how do I know?" The answer will help you determine if your thought is based on something real or imagined. If you find that you assume this, you can clearly name it as an assumption and not as a fact. You disputed the negative thought that your boss is planning to fire you. If you determine that the source of your negative thought is external or based on a fact such as, "My boss told me that he is planning to fire me," you may then explore possibilities for dealing with that reality.

Break the grip of rumination: Rumination is when something happens and you go over and over it again in your mind but don't get anywhere. You keep asking yourself questions without finding any answers. The first step to break the grip of rumination is to create awareness by recognizing that you are ruminating and that it isn't helpful. The next step is to engage in a healthy and joyful distraction, such as a walk in nature, swimming, biking, calling or meeting a friend or something else that will fully absorb you, lift your mood and break the grip of rumination. Then, with a much clearer mind about your adverse situation, you are in a better mental state to dispute your negative thoughts and address whatever problem you face. I personally use journaling to gain awareness of and clarity about my ruminating thoughts and to dispute them.

Dealing with negative people: Ask yourself if there are people who are a major source of negativity in your life. These are people who, when you interact with them, drain your energy or make you feel miserable. This might be because they complain a lot or frequently make negative comments. For example, when you are enthusiastic about something, they react in a way that is critical, pessimistic or even sarcastic. There are two choices: You can avoid the person or make them change their negative behavior.

Avoiding means that you decide to spend as little time with that person as necessary or no time at all. You can try to make them change their negativity by giving them feedback about their behavior and the effect it has on you or others, the way I did with the two members of my team. I realize that giving negative feedback can be difficult. It is important to set the context for the conversation. That means making a request for a conversation, making sure that the time and location allow for a private conversation without distraction and also sharing that it is about an important topic you want to discuss. Be aware that the person might not be aware of their negativity and the effect it has. I suggest sharing your positive intent, focusing on the behavior, not the person, and sharing the effect the behavior has. When the person acknowledges the issue, you can then make a request for change.

When I coached Kyle (name changed), a sales executive whose boss was always negative in his approach with his sales team, he eventually shared with his boss how he and his team experienced the boss's behavior and that every time it happened, it crushed the team's morale. To Kyle's surprise, although he had feared that his boss would react angrily, his boss was instead open to the feedback and acknowledged the issue. He sincerely thanked him for it. When Kyle then made a request to change his behavior, his boss willingly committed to it. Kyle, who had felt uncomfortable about giving feedback to his boss, afterward felt more empowered to face and influence negative behavior of others.

Create distance: This is a situation where you have reacted negatively. Take a moment to reflect on that negative moment, and ask yourself if the negativity you felt was really necessary. Look carefully at the circumstances, and assess how you feel about it now. There's a good chance that after some time has passed, you feel differently and the negativity you previously felt may be reduced or even gone. Approach this exercise in a mood of curiosity and interest and with the aspiration to grow. As in the previous exercise, you might even feel amused about how little reason there was to slip into negativity.

Create recovery periods: While our need for recovery periods seems obvious, this is not something we practice well, as the astronomically high number of unused vacation days in the United States shows. To build resilience, you need both shorter periods of relaxation during your workday and recovery activities outside of work. Combine these times of relaxation with activities that bring joy, which is the emotion associated with a desire to celebrate life and to continue living. In such a state, we savor the moment and feel pleasure, delight and are more energetic. It brings a smile to our face, and others observe our inner glow. What brings joy and is relaxing may be different from person to person. For example, for me, it includes winding down at the end of a workday with a relaxed family dinner and joyful conversations, reading a good book before going to bed, journaling and exercising in the morning, preferably in nature, family vacations in a relaxed environment and spending quality time with good friends. If you haven't yet, I encourage you to create your own recovery times and activities.

Use a powerful mantra: In moments of near failure, when we're at risk of giving up, having a powerful, easy-to-recall mantra can focus our energy on recovering from that failure. I learned this from a great mentor in resilience, my father. I never saw him quit when he faced adversities in the pursuit of something important to him. As a young man, I adopted this as my own mantra for challenging times. "Never quit!" For me, this mantra was associated with pride and hope. No one can stop you from rebounding unless you give up. I encourage you to find your own mantra that you can recall in difficult times. Let me caution, however, to only use a mantra like this in pursuit of worthy goals, never a senseless activity that risks anyone's well-being or even life.

Connecting to Others

Another important source of both negativity and positivity is the people in our lives. Following are three practices that help to feed positive emotions. They include kind connections, joyful connections and coaching.

Kind connections: We humans are social beings and connections with others can give us energy if the interaction is positive or deplete our energy if the interaction is negative. Practicing kindness has an enormous effect on the positive mood of the relationship. Cultivating empathy, compassion and interest enables behaviors such as caring, serving and understanding that will be perceived by others as kindness.

Joyful connections: Creating joyful experiences together is a way to increase positivity. For example, when I invited my global teams for planning retreats, I always made sure we planned time to do something joyful together. I could observe how this lifted the mood of the whole team, not only during the fun activity but also the next day when we continued our planning meeting. The elevated mood from the night before carried over to the next day and helped to create positive relationships in the long term.

Coaching: When you feel stuck in a moment of setback, change or adversity, coaching can help you see new possibilities for action and shift to emotions of hope and optimism. A coach, when appropriately trained and experienced, can help you recognize negative thought patterns and moods and shift to thoughts and emotions that are more helpful in your specific situation. Even if you don't have access to a professional coach, reaching out and talking to a friend, mentor or advisor can give you new perspectives and create a positive emotional shift.

An example of such an emotional shift happened to Jamie (name changed). One day Jamie called me and shared that she had been laid off from the software company where she had worked as a project manager. She asked if I could coach her to find a new job. The reason for her layoff was that her company had decided to outsource the development work her team had been doing to the lower-cost economy of another country. Legally, her employer had followed all the rules. But that didn't make her feel any better. Jamie said, "I had put my heart and soul into this company, and from one day to the next they didn't need me anymore."

The loss of her job was painful, and Jamie was experiencing a mix of negative emotions, including fear about not finding another job like this, sadness about her loss, shame about being out of work even though it was not her fault. But the emotion that appeared to be the most powerful in our conversation was resentment. She complained that what had happened to her was unfair and repeated this throughout our conversation. Resentment is the emotion associated with being a victim of someone's actions that we perceive as unfair. On one hand, Jamie needed some time to grieve her loss and go through all the negative emotions that come with that process. On the other hand, I noticed that staying in resentment too long wouldn't allow her to look forward.

In subsequent coaching sessions, I allowed time and space for her to grieve, but also focused on creating an emotional shift away from the resentment that kept her thoughts spinning in the past. I encouraged her to shift toward feeling optimism so she could see and pursue new possibilities for the future. In Chapter 4, I shared that a shift from resentment to optimism is enabled by shifting to acceptance first, as described in the *"Accept and face reality"* practice above. That's why I guided Jamie through a process of accepting the fact that she had lost her old job as something that she cannot change, no matter how often she is ruminating about how unfair this is. Something magical happens when we accept what happened in the past. It opens up the possibility of shifting to emotions associated with the future, such as optimism. And that is what Jamie was able to achieve. It relieved her of the negativity of constantly thinking about what had happened to her, and she was able to recover from her job loss and redirect her focus to her future.

Connecting to Creativity

Connecting to creativity in moments of adversity or setback enables us to shift from negative emotions such as frustration, fear or anger to positive emotions such as interest, inspiration or hope. That shift makes us more resilient. While there are many ways to connect to creativity, one practice is called *bricolage*, which psychologists call the ability to improvise a solution to a problem with whatever tools and materials are at hand.

I learned about the practice of bricolage from Gene Kranz, who was the lead flight director in Houston during NASA's Apollo 13 manned moon landing mission at a session with other leaders from my company. Kranz shared that he was on duty at the Houston command center when part of the Apollo 13 service module exploded. Soon after the explosion, it became clear to him and his team that without finding a solution to repair the damage quickly, the three astronauts could not survive the mission. Kranz immediately instructed his team of engineers at the Houston command center to find a fix that could be created from materials available to the astronauts on board Apollo 13. They found a solution and then remotely guided the three astronauts to recreate it in their craft's service module. The engineering team's practice of bricolage in Houston allowed the three astronauts to return to Earth safely.

Bricolage is one way to connect to creativity in times of adversity that helps build resilience. Additional ideas may include building something new, composing music, solving a puzzle, writing poetry or painting a picture. Maybe it's something you once liked but gave up doing because of other priorities. As an example, many years ago I rediscovered my passion for writing, which I'd given up after I had finished high school. Today, this is one of my major sources of joy, interest, inspiration, hope and other positive emotions. Whenever I go through a challenging time, I can count on journaling to help me create a positive shift. I have heard many similar experiences from people who have found their own creative outlet.

Connecting to the Magic of Life

Opening ourselves up to the magic of life, such as observing a child lost in play or a bird lifting off a branch, may put us in awe, capture our interest, inspire us to act and even create hope.

A powerful example is the performance of Shostakovich's Seventh Symphony during the siege by Hitler's army of Leningrad during World War II. On August 9, 1942, in the besieged city, an orchestra comprised of the last surviving musicians, nursed back from starvation, performed Dimitri Shostakovich's Seventh Symphony. Ravaged by hunger and surrounded by death after nearly a year of siege, audience members had traded their meager daily bread ration for tickets to the performance. The music from the concert hall could be heard over loudspeakers throughout the city—and even by the German soldiers at the front line.

People listened with closed eyes, and when it was finished, first there was silence; then the audience rose and erupted into thundering applause. The players turned and embraced one another. Witnesses recalled that hearing the music brought them back to life. While the siege went on for another year and a half, the performance of this symphony is remembered as a turning point of the siege on Leningrad. Hearing this music aroused in the people the emotions of awe, gratitude, joy, pride, hope, inspiration and, above all, love for their city, as author M.T. Anderson describes in *Symphony for the City of the Dead*. Despite tremendous adversity and suffering, evoking and maintaining these positive emotions helped Leningraders be resilient and reclaim their city step-by-step and finally overcome Hitler's evil plan to starve the people of Leningrad to death.

Positivity Clearly Is a Choice

Coming back to my own experience during the early days of the pandemic, I reminded myself that positivity is a choice, and I committed to following practices that allowed me to use some of the sources of positivity explained above.

First, I reconnected to my purpose in life, which is to help evolve humanity and create a positive future for all. Recalling this shifted me into the positive emotions of empathy, compassion and interest.

Second, I created a routine of neglected practices, including meditating, practicing yoga, journaling, reflective reading and exercising in nature. Luckily, I found a beautiful park that had not been closed. I love old trees and the life they host. There I spent time and opened myself to the magic of nature. I also became extra mindful about contributing to the positivity in my family, such as listening with interest or just appreciating the humor we share together.

One night, with a twinkle in my eyes, I asked my wife, "How have I been doing?" "What do you mean?" she asked. "Did I spread positivity or negativity during the day?" Grateful for my conscious effort, with a smile, she said to me, "You did well!" and we all laughed together. Our amusement was infectious, and I believe it was one more positive emotion we cultivated that helped us as a family to become more resilient in this unprecedented time. Positivity clearly is a choice!

I encourage you to revisit the previously described sources of positivity whenever you feel the need for increasing your positivity ratio. You may then select and focus on the practices that speak most to you. From my own experience, I know that developing positivity and resilience is a lifelong pursuit because life's demands on us change constantly and without any warning and time to prepare.

Let's summarize the key learnings about the seventh essential leadership competency of practicing positivity and being resilient.

Summary:

- ✓ Change, setbacks and adversity are a normal part of life. Expecting otherwise will make you slip into negativity and affect your resilience.

- ✓ Resilience is your ability to recover from setbacks, adapt well to change and keep going in the face of adversity.

- ✓ You can build resilience by increasing your positivity ratio—defined as the amount of positivity relative to your amount of negativity. I suggest a positivity ratio of five or higher to build your resilience.

- ✓ Positive emotions include the six essential emotions from the previous Chapters 1–6 in the ASPIRE Leadership Model—empathy, compassion, interest, optimism, inspiration and trust—and others, such as aspiration, amusement, awe, enthusiasm, gratitude, hope, joy, peace, love, pride and serenity.

✓ Practices that can help you shift out of negative toward positive emotions may focus on identifying and influencing the sources of negativity, such as negative thought patterns or negative people, and connecting to sources of positivity, such as purpose, self, others, creativity or the magic of life.

✓ Because negative emotions are alerting us to something of importance that is affecting our life, blocking or suppressing them will backfire as it multiplies the misery. Instead, we must learn to become aware of them and understand and manage their source.

✓ As the leader, you greatly affect the mood (positively or negatively) of your team, organization or community. Creating a culture of positivity is of utmost importance for building resilience for yourself and in your team, organization or community.

Pause and Reflect

Before you continue reading, I recommend pausing a moment and doing this simple self-test by reflecting:

What was your ratio of positivity over negativity in your interactions during the last 24 hours with others or in your own inner dialogue?

Positivity:

1...2...3...4...5...6...7...8...9...10

If your positivity is lower than five, ask yourself, "What is the typical source of my negativity?" "What is my biggest barrier to positivity?" and, "What sources of positivity could I connect to, and what could I practice to create a positive shift?"

Now that we have addressed the seven essential leadership behaviors for creating positive change and the emotions that drive those behaviors, the following Conclusion will reflect on the personal transformation that may occur when practicing these behaviors and emotions.

"Each of us individually has an effect on the lives of beings around us through the quiet processes going on in our minds. If we are full of good feelings, they radiate around us and people want to be near. If we are full of bad feelings, others tend to stay away. So if we would be activists for good, for the positive, we must assume responsibility for our minds as well as our speech and our physical activities, otherwise our negative mental habits will drag down the entire community of beings. On the other hand, when we break through into the liberty of the heart, mind and spirit in the process of enlightenment, we free others at the same time."

~ *Robert A.F. Thurman*

CONCLUSION

Now that we have explored in detail each of the seven essential emotions and behaviors of the ASPIRE Leadership Model in Chapters 1–7, let's do a brief recap of the model itself. This includes who it is for, the model itself, its benefits, application with other leadership models and where to go from here.

Leading Change from Where You Are

Emotions brought down the Berlin Wall, sealed Germany's reunification, enabled the peaceful transition to democracy in South Africa, won civil rights in the U.S. and even moved members of the Ku Klux Klan to give up their robes. Emotions also allowed entrepreneurs like Traci to mobilize people to launch and grow a new business and fueled people's resilience during the global COVID-19 pandemic.

In all of these cases, empathy, compassion, interest, optimism, inspiration, trust and positivity served as drivers for the leadership behaviors that created aspirational change.

But emotions can also be a barrier to the behavior required for leading such change, such as Jennifer's contempt and distrust that demotivated her team.

As these and other examples throughout the book show, *the seven essential emotions and leadership behaviors* empower you to lead change no matter where you are—at home, in your community, your organization, your school or wherever your place may be in society.

Who This Book Is For

The ASPIRE Leadership Model is for leaders and changemakers who want to create positive, aspirational change no matter their role or level in an organization or in society. This means that while you may be a formal leader when creating change, leading change does not require that you be one. If you aspire to create change, are able to envision a new future and influence people to change their behavior so that your vision becomes a reality, then you are a leader.

The Seven Emotions and Behaviors

A useful model in the context of influencing behavior is to think of emotions as drivers of or barriers to the desired behavior. This means that the ability to understand your own emotional barriers and drivers and those of others is essential for changing your own behavior and influencing a change in the behavior of others. Because there are more than 250 emotions, and a person can experience a mixture of emotions at any given time, learning emotions can seem overwhelming. That's why the ASPIRE Leadership Model focuses on the seven essential emotions for leading positive, aspirational change.

The emotional competencies of Chapters 1–3—empathy, compassion and interest—help you with caring about, committing to serving and understanding people's needs and issues better.

These first three competencies lay the foundation for the next three emotional competencies of Chapters 4–6—optimism, inspiration and trust. Optimism helps you envision a future in which the needs of the people you care about are fully met, and the issues related to meeting those needs are resolved. Inspiration helps you mobilize people and trust helps you coordinate effective actions to make your vision a reality.

Finally, once you are on your journey toward making your vision a reality, even the best planning may not prepare you for all the adversities that can get in the way of reaching your goals. Adversities are a normal part of life. That's why the final of the seven essential behavioral competencies addressed in Chapter 7 is resilience. Positivity helps to build resilience and it can be learned. Unlike the previous six emotions, positivity consists of a pallet of emotions, such as awe, gratitude or joy.

Benefits – How a Leader May Transform

In teaching the seven emotional and behavioral competencies of this model to various types of leaders, including those in startups, midsize companies, large corporations, non-profit organizations or communities, I have observed over the years that when people practice these competencies, they not only create change in the world around them but also a transformation in consciousness in themselves.

That's what happened for Srini, a leader I've coached on the seven essential emotions and behaviors through his work as first-line manager of a small team in a midsize IT service firm to his role as senior executive at a large Fortune 500 company.

When asked about the benefits of learning and practicing the competencies represented in the ASPIRE Leadership Model, he told me:

"I have become a different person than I was when I started out learning about these emotions and behaviors."

When I asked how he is different now, he said:

"Before, when I was facing a challenging situation, I was allowing myself to spiral into a negative mood without being aware of it."

I asked Srini, "Can you describe more about what that was like?"

"Well, one time someone hurt me, and I felt the urge to react vengefully. Feeling like that usually got me ruminating about how unfairly I was treated. The problem was, being stuck in the past didn't allow me to look beyond myself, and it kept me from truly leading others."

Our greatest challenge with other people is that we often don't see the problem with our own behavior and blame the situations we encounter on the beliefs and behaviors of others. That becomes particularly evident in a more and more divided world, whether those divisions arise in our overall society, in our communities or in our organizations or workplace, such as Srini had experienced in the past. I suggest that learning and practicing the seven essential emotions of leading positive, aspirational change will drive behaviors that enable leaders to overcome the divisions, no matter where they aspire to create change.

Next, I asked Srini how he feels now.

"Now, I am very conscious of how I feel in a specific situation, and when I feel a certain negative emotion, I use it to understand what story is going through my mind. I can then dispute or validate my story and create a shift that is more helpful in dealing with the situation."

I wanted to know more and asked Srini, "How has that changed you?"

"I feel transformed into a better human being at home, in my community and at work. I recognized this in the way people react more positively toward me than they did before. As a result, I have been able to increase my circle of influence steadily. For example, I used to lead a team of a handful of people, and I felt nervous. Now, even though I am leading a much larger organization, I feel confident about it."

Srini's example shows that we can learn to become aware of our emotions and create a conscious emotional shift within us that will support the leadership behaviors most needed in a specific situation. Cultivating empathy, compassion and interest made him care about, serve and understand others much better. He was then able to help create an emotional shift in others to influence their behavior positively.

Srini's example also shows that over time, we can widen our circles of empathy, compassion, interest, optimism, inspiration, trust and positivity to include more and more individuals, thereby influencing and creating an aspirational future for wider and wider circles of people. In Srini's case, that circle widened from a handful of people to nearly a thousand within just a couple of years.

Application with Other Leadership Models

Both I and many leaders I work with have been trained in and are using other leadership models. In the examples I've encountered, the ASPIRE Leadership Model complements and enhances other leadership models. The reason is that the other models usually focus more on the leader's behaviors and less on the emotions that drive them. Knowing which of the seven essential emotions to apply, and when, makes the other models more effective.

The appendix offers three examples: the SLII® Model for leading people, the Competing Values Framework for leading cultural change and the Blue Earth Model © for leading innovation. There you can read a brief introduction to each of the three leadership models and how the seven essential emotions of the ASPIRE Leadership Model enhance their effectiveness and when to apply them.

Where to Go from Here

Learning the seven essential emotions and behaviors is not "an all or nothing" decision. I have observed that after practicing just one or two of the seven emotions, people were showing behaviors that made them more effective in leading change.

Following are specific actions you can take to continue your learning or support the learning of others.

1. Revisit your self-assessments in each of Chapters 1–7, and select the emotion you rated lowest and for which you have the greatest need. Follow the best practices that speak to you in the related chapter. Repeat this process for each of the seven emotions.

2. Follow me on linkedin.com/in/reinerlomb for upcoming online sessions, podcasts or blog posts about the ASPIRE Leadership Model.

3. If reading ASPIRE has made you wonder, "What is it I'm passionate about changing in my life or in the world?" you can explore more about this in *The Boomerang Approach* at reinerlomb.com/books.

4. If you have questions about your learning journey, inquiries about workshops for your organization, speaking at your events or executive coaching, visit reinerlomb.com/contact.

A final observation. Learning and practicing the seven essential emotions for leading positive, aspirational change is a lifelong journey. Progress on that journey can be measured by the size of ever-expanding circles of empathy, compassion, interest, optimism, inspiration, trust and positivity that will allow you to influence more and more people as a leader.

As you cultivate them, these emotions will also become stepping stones to greater and greater self-awareness and consciousness, and with these comes greater spiritual growth. For me spirituality means finding meaning in our existence. Self-interest is a major barrier in finding meaning because it separates us from others and the world. The seven essential emotions help us transcend self-interest and connect us to others and self in a new and deeper way. For me, that is spiritual growth.

Appendix: Applying the ASPIRE Model with Other Leadership Models

Many useful leadership models have been created to help leaders create change, and you may already be trained in or using one or more of them. The various models focus on different levels of leadership, including self, others (individual or team), organization or larger-scale change, such as creating whole new products or ideas that disrupt and transform the way we live or society itself.

Each of the seven leadership behaviors and emotions can be used by itself but also in combination with any of these leadership models. They greatly enhance their effectiveness and therefore your effectiveness as a leader. The following are three examples of leadership and change models designed for three different levels: others, organization and society.

- *Leading people* according to their level of development

  Model: SLII® Model

- *Leading cultural change* of a team or organization

  Model: Competing Values Framework

- *Leading innovation*

  Model: Blue Earth Model ©

Applying the Competencies to Other Leadership and Change Models

1. Leading People: The SLII® Model

The SLII® Model has been designed for leaders to manage the performance of each individual team member according to that member's level of development. It distinguishes four levels of development (D1-D4) of a team member and the associated leadership style (S1-S4) of the manager to achieve the optimal performance of that person as shown in the table below. The third column shows the emotions you should pay special attention to for each level of development and associated leadership style. This does not mean that the other emotions not mentioned for a specific level of development and leadership style are not important. For example, trust is always important in any collaborative relationship, as are empathy, compassion and interest as the emotional drivers for caring, serving and understanding.

Level of Development		Leadership Style		Emotional Drivers
D1	Enthusiastic Beginner	S1	Directing	Compassion and Positivity
D2	Disillusioned Learner	S2	Coaching	Empathy and Inspiration

| D3 | Capable but Cautious Performer | S3 | Supporting | Interest and Self-Trust |
| D4 | Self-Reliant Achiever | S4 | Delegating | Trust and Optimism |

The ***Enthusiastic Beginner*** is hopeful, curious, enthusiastic and optimistic but unskilled. This means that he or she comes with a lot of positive energy but needs clear directions in the form of priorities, plans, teaching, showing, checking, monitoring and feedback. Because of this close hand-holding approach, the leader must have an absolute commitment for developing others, which requires compassion. The trials and errors required for learning the new skills may create frustrations in the leader, and staying in a positive emotional state is absolutely critical for the resilience needed in the learning process.

The ***Disillusioned Learner*** is overwhelmed, confused, demotivated, demoralized and frustrated while having flashes of competence. Thus, he or she needs a coaching approach which includes exploring and asking, explaining and clarifying, redirecting, sharing feedback, encouraging and praising. The leader must be able to identify the underlying barriers to learning and therefore be very empathetic, but also needs to be inspirational in order to reignite in the person a passion for learning.

The *Capable but Cautious Performer* is very self-critical, cautious, doubtful, insecure, bored and apathetic, but is capable and is contributing. So he or she needs a more supporting leadership style, which includes asking questions, listening, reassuring, facilitating self-reliant problem-solving, collaborating, encouraging feedback and appreciation. This requires the leader to develop a real interest in the stories that drive the self-critical behavior and self-doubt of the person so that he can help the person reshape the stories in a more beneficial way. Helping the person develop self-trust will be key. In order to help the person overcome feeling bored and apathetic, the leader can also help uncover what it is that would fuel the person's interest and align it with the role.

The *Self-Reliant Achiever* is justifiably confident, consistently competent, inspired and inspires, self-assured and self-directed. What this person needs from the leader is trust, empowerment, acknowledgment, affirmation and challenges. This requires the leader to share a vision that is grounded in optimism and challenging at the same time and trust that he or she will know what to do to help the team advance toward that vision.

2. Leading Cultural Change – The Competing Values Framework

Values and beliefs drive our thoughts and emotions, which then drive our behaviors. While the ASPIRE Leadership Model focuses on emotions as drivers of leadership behavior, this section applies the seven emotional competencies to "the dominant framework in the world for assessing organizational culture," the *Competing Values Framework,* which was originally developed by Robert E. Quinn and John Rohrbaugh, and looks at values as drivers of behavior. It distinguishes four dominant sets of values that drive people's behaviors in organizations which are labeled as CONTROL (red), COLLABORATE (yellow), CREATE (green) and COMPETE (blue). The image below shows a simplified version of the *Competing Values Framework*, mapping the primary emotions that fuel the behaviors aligned with the specific values represented by each quadrant.

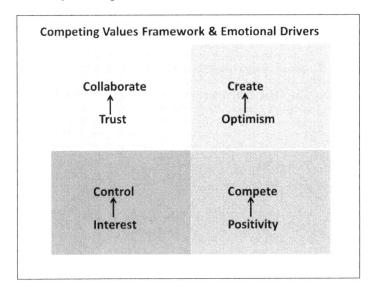

Control: An organizational culture that is compatible with this form values stability, predictability, efficiency and is internally driven. In such an organization, effective leaders are good coordinators and organizers. The control leader creates order out of chaos by putting structures in place and maintaining or increasing efficiency of the whole system in incremental steps. Because they need to understand the complexities, interdependencies and details of an organizational system, they must be driven by their *interest* in understanding, building and optimizing that system. (See Chapter 3.)

Create: An organizational culture that is compatible with this form values flexibility, risk-taking by embracing uncertainty, fostering innovation and creativity and is externally driven. In such an organization, effective leaders are visionary entrepreneurs or intrapreneurs. The *"create" leader* must be able to see, create and pursue an aspirational vision for the organization and therefore be *optimistic*. (See Chapter 4.) This leader must mobilize the organization and therefore *inspire* the stakeholders.

Compete: An organizational culture that is compatible with this form values winning, is customer (externally) focused and results-driven. In such an organization, leaders are market-driven, constantly trying to outpace the competition and to gain market share. In such a fast-paced and constantly changing environment, the *"compete" leader* (and the organization) must be resilient and therefore maintain the need to cultivate *positivity*. (See Chapter 7.)

Collaborate: An organizational culture that is compatible with this form values teamwork, consensus and employee participation and development. It's based on the leadership philosophy that if an organization takes care of its people, it will take care of its customers. It aims at stability and is more internally focused. In such a culture, people share a lot about themselves and empathy, compassion for and interest in each other are high. In such a (collaborative) environment, the *"collaborate" leader* (and the organization) must create and nurture a high degree of *trust*. (See Chapter 6.)

Leaders (and organizations) who hold the opposite values of the CONTROL and CREATE quadrant are in a natural conflict; so are the leaders (and organizations) who hold the opposite values of the COMPETE and COLLABORATE quadrant. Imagine the chaos a *create leader* causes threatening the order that the *control leader* tries to maintain and the frustration that the resistance to change of the *control leader* causes in the *create leader*. In the same way, the *compete leader* can easily ruffle feathers with the *collaborate leader* and vice versa. Similar conflicts occur between the compete leaders and control leaders and the create and collaborate leaders because of their external versus internal focus. In my experience, these conflicts are solvable and can even be transformed into a synergistic win-win partnership by applying the behavioral and emotional leadership competencies of the ASPIRE Leadership Model. Let's recall the following conflict from Chapter 1.

Gary, the hard-driving sales manager (compete leader) of a midsized manufacturing company, is trying to convince Samantha, head of manufacturing (control leader), into a commitment of manufacturing a million units of a new product by the end of next month. To pressure her to agree, Gary tells Samantha, "We will only win this deal if I can go back to the client with this commitment."

But Samantha, whose performance is measured by product quality and meeting her unit commitment (versus Gary, who is measured on revenue) says, "Gary, that is impossible! Producing that many units so quickly won't leave enough time for quality control. I will not commit to that."

Gary, operating in full drive mode, now feels threatened that he is going to lose this big deal. He shifts into the threat system, bursts out in anger and says something offensive to Samantha.

Samantha now feels attacked and shifts into the threat system. She is not only trying to protect the company from making a commitment she thinks it can't fulfill—or could even be sued for—but also protect her own reputation in her professional role. Both leave the call feeling resentment toward the other, which blocks any kind of creative and collaborative conversation they might have to find a solution.

Now imagine an alternative conversation in which Gary and Samantha are making an effort to become aware of the conflicting values their roles hold. They achieve that by postponing judgment, assuming positive intentions of the other person and trying to put themselves in the other person's shoes. By doing that, Gary is now able to ask in a calm tone, "Samantha, what keeps you from making that commitment?" Samantha explains that she is afraid that she wouldn't be able to fulfill the commitment, and the subsequent damage for their company would be costly, and it may even cost her job. Gary responds, "I can understand your hesitation now. What can I do to help you?" Samantha responds, "I understand how important that deal is for you and would like us to win it too. What other options do you think we have to still win the deal?"

Now they have shifted from operating in the drive and threat system to the soothing system. Mutual empathy allows them to understand what is in the way of making the deal happen and allows them to jointly come up with ideas on how to overcome these barriers. As the conversation continues, they come to an agreement to meet jointly with the customer to understand the real customer needs behind this request and discuss alternative delivery options. In the meeting the customer appreciates the manufacturer's commitment to quality and offers some flexibility about the delivery schedule. Gary and Samantha, by collaborating, are able to work out a schedule that allows them to win the deal without jeopardizing quality. It's win-win for Gary and Samantha.

In this scenario, Gary and Samantha value the differences in their roles and associated values. Using emotional competence, such as empathy, compassion and interest, they bridge their value conflict and create a synergistic partnership that has the potential to create many wins for the company and meet the needs of its clients. Building on their initial success together, they may develop optimism about future possibilities and trust in each other. Overcoming their resentment by accepting their different roles and associated values also opens the door to develop and nurture positivity in their relationship, which will make them more resilient when facing challenges together. In this scenario, as a team, they create a cultural shift, embracing all four quadrants of the conflicting values framework and by doing so create the effectiveness of their organization.

3. Leading Innovation – Blue Earth Model ©

The Blue Earth Model ©, developed by Udaiyan Jatar, integrates the process, tools and skills to *discover, invent and scale* transformative solutions. It is based on the principles of successful social movements, such as transforming civil rights (MLK) or dismantling empires (Gandhi) and Transcendent Brands©, such as Apple, Nike or others. A transcendent brand cannot be commoditized because its customers remain loyal based on a deep emotional connection with the brand. To create this deep emotional connection, the Blue Earth Model © follows the following three phases:

I.   Unfiltered Discovery

- Discover the stakeholders' highest aspirations.
- Create the organization's true purpose.
- Identify the barriers to behavior change.

II.   Crafting Transformation

- Create a transformative value proposition.
- Define and validate behavior change.
- Design and prototype innovative solutions.

III. Scaling Impact

- Scale by following the adoption curve.
- Develop leaders coherent with the desired behavior change.
- Create a go-to-market model and communication coherent with the desired behavior change.

Embedded in this process is a scientific approach to changing and scaling human behavior because in the end, successful innovation means changing people's behavior at scale. The seven behavioral and emotional leadership competencies of the ASPIRE Leadership Model support the behavior-change approach to innovation and transformation of the Blue Earth Model ©. The following mapping shows which and where the seven behavioral and emotional competencies should be applied in the Blue Earth process.

Blue Earth Model ©	Emotional Drivers
I. Unfiltered Discovery • Discovering the stakeholders' highest aspirations. • Creating the organization's true purpose (vision). • Identifying the barriers to behavior change.	• *Trust* to allow the stakeholders to be open and vulnerable. • *Empathy and Interest* to listen to and understand the stakeholders' highest aspirations and their barriers for behavior change. • *Compassion* and *Optimism* to develop the organization's true purpose (vision) aligned with the stakeholders' highest aspirations.
II. Crafting Transformation • Create a transformative value proposition. • Define and validate behavior change.	• *Empathy* to understand the drivers and barriers of the stakeholders' behaviors. • *Interest* in understanding the psychology of behavior change and how to apply it to create a transformative value proposition and designing

• Design and prototype innovative solutions.	and prototyping innovative solutions. • *Empathy and compassion* in designing and testing the prototypes.
III. Scaling Impact • Scale by following the adoption curve. • Develop leaders coherent with the desired behavior change. • Create a go-to-market model and communication coherent with the desired behavior change.	• *Empathy, compassion* for and *interest* in the needs of stakeholders along the adoption curve. • *Inspiration* to mobilize people. • *Trust* to coordinate effective action. • *Positivity* to fuel resilience to overcome the obstacles on the bumpy road to scale the adoption of the solution.

Emotions That Overcome Homelessness

The ways in which these emotions helped to transform behavior in the fight against homelessness were observable during a Blue Earth consulting project with the Atlanta Center for Self Sufficiency (ACSS). The Blue Earth Model © was applied to develop an innovative approach that would help people who were homeless find and keep work and stay off the street. Previous programs had focused on getting people an apartment and finding them a paying job. With that approach of focusing only on meeting people's basic needs, after three months, more than 50% of the people had dropped out of their jobs and ended up back on the street.

In contrast, Blue Earth's approach focused on looking at the people not as homeless who just needed to meet their basic needs, but as human beings with aspirations and passions like everybody else. The approach focused on empathy, compassion, building trust and a deep interest in understanding people's human needs.

For example, Angelique (name change), who had not held a steady job for a long time and had been forced to live on the street had, since her childhood, dreamed of becoming an airline pilot because she was passionate about airplanes. While becoming a pilot at that stage of her life was not realistic, the new ACSS program helped her to find a job where she could be around the airplanes she was so passionate about. That inspired Angelique to get out of bed every morning and go to her new job. By helping people find jobs that were aligned with their aspirations and passions as much as possible, more than 75% of the previously homeless felt inspired to remain in their jobs after nine months.

Creating work that people were passionate about with a sense of purpose made the difference in their staying employed and off the street.

Applying the Competencies to Other Models

The previous mapping of the seven competencies is meant to provide examples to inspire you to apply the seven competencies of the ASPIRE Leadership Model to your own favorite leadership or change model. In our experience, simply applying one or two of the seven competencies can increase the effectiveness of your model and your own effectiveness as a leader in creating change. Then, over time, you can incrementally add other competencies.

Bibliography

Following is a list of resources that are cited or that have inspired me in writing ASPIRE. The resources are listed in the order of the chapters to which they relate. Some resources relate to more than one chapter and are listed more than once.

Preface: The Intangible Force

Aurich, H. G. (2006). *Heinz Eisfeld, Sächsische Lebensbilder, Band 6*, Stuttgart

Fuehrer, C. (2008). *Und wir sind dabei gewesen, Die Revolution, die aus der Kirche kam,* Ullstein Buchverlag GmbH, Berlin

Haase-Hindenburg, G. (2007). *Der Mann, der die Mauer oeffnete.* Wilhelm Heyne Verlag, Muenchen.

Lomb, R. (2014). *The Boomerang Approach: Return to Purpose, Ignite Your Passion.*

Introduction: Seven Essential Emotions to Lead Change

Quinn, Robert E. (1996). *Deep Change: Discovering the Leader Within.* Jossey-Bass Publishers, California.

Grenny, J., et al. (2013). *Influencer: The New Science of Leading Change.* McGraw-Hill Education.

Friedman, T. (2016). *Thank You for Being Late: An Optimist's Guide To Thriving In he Age of Acceleration*, Farrar, Straus and Giroux, New York

Goleman, D. (1995). *Emotional Intelligence: Why It Can Matter More Than IQ.* A Bantam Book

Newby, D., Nuñez, L. (2017). *The Unopened Gift: A Primer in Emotional Literacy.*

Feldman Barrett, L. (2018). *How Emotions Are Made: The Secret Life of the Brain.* First Mariner Books edition, Houghton Mifflin Harcourt Publishing Company, New York

Pinchot, G. III. (1985). *Intrapreneuring: Why You Don't Have to Leave the Corporation to Become an Entrepreneur.* Harper & Row Publishers, New York

Goleman, D., Boyatzis, R., McKee, A. (2013). *Primal Leadership.* Harvard Business Review Press, Boston

Scharmer, C. O. (2018). *The Essentials of Theory U, Core Principles and Applications,* Barrett-Koehler Publishers, Inc., Oakland

Chapter 1: Empathy – The Gate to Caring

Greenleaf, R. K. (1977). *Servant Leadership: A Journey into the Nature of Legitimate Power of Greatness.* Paulist Press.

Goleman, D. (2017). Emotional Intelligence: Empathy. *Harvard Business Review Press.*

Gilbert, P., Ph.D., Choden. (2014). *Mindful Compassion: How the Science of Compassion Can Help You Understand Your Emotions, Live in the Present, and connect deeply with others.* New Harbinger Publications.

Solomon, L. (2017). Becoming Powerful Makes You Less Empathetic (based on research by Keltner, Dacher). Empathy, *Harvard Review Press.*

Lomb, R. (2015). Catching the Dream of the Ute Mountain Ute Tribe—A Glimmer of Hope in a Native 'National Emergency.' *Huffpost.*

Lomb, R. (2017). Lack of Empathy Drives Destructive Leadership Behavior – Uber CEO Admits He Must Change. *Huffpost.*

Chapter 2: Compassion – The Commitment to Serving

Greenleaf, R. K. (1977). *Servant Leadership, A Journey into the Nature of Legitimate Power of Greatness.* Paulist Press.

Armstrong, K. (2011). *Twelve Steps to a Compassionate Life.* Anchor Books.

Wright, R. (2009). "The Evolution of Compassion." TEDSalon.

Gilbert, P., Ph.D., Choden. (2014). *Mindful Compassion: how the science of compassion can help you understand your emotions, live in the present, and connect deeply with others.* New Harbinger Publications.

Camus, A. (1991). *The Plague.* First Vintage International Edition.

Weng, H. Y., Fox, A. S., Shackman, A. J., et al. (2013). Compassion Training Alters Altruism and Neural Responses to Suffering.

Neff, K., Ph.D. (2011). *Self Compassion: the Proven Power of Being Kind to Yourself.* William Morrow.

Lomb, R. (2017). Lead with Compassion: A New Approach to Reconcile the Country, *Huffpost.*

Chapter 3: Interest – The Drive to Understanding

Ornstein, M. (Director). (2016). *Accidental Courtesy: Daryl Davis, Race & America.*

Renninger, K. A., Hidi, S. E. (2016). *The Power of Interest for Motivation and Engagement.* Routledge Taylor & Francis Group.

Silvia, P. J. (2008). Interest – The Curious Emotion. University of North Carolina

Newby, D., Nuñez, L. (2017). *The Unopened Gift: A Primer in Emotional Literacy.*

Keltner, D. (2016). Why Do We Feel Awe? *Greater Good Magazine.*

Lomb, R. (2017). Leaders Must Understand and Empathize with People's Needs to Defeat Radical Fear- and Anger-Mongering. *Huffpost.*

Scharmer, C. O. (2018). *The Essentials of Theory U: Core Principles and Applications.* Barrett-Koehler Publishers Inc.

Chapter 4: Optimism – The Lens for Visioning

Fuehrer, C. (2008). *Und wir sind dabei gewesen, Die Revolution, die aus der Kirche kam.* Ullstein Buchverlag GmbH.

Patterson, T. (2009). Europe's Revolution: The pastor who brought down the Berlin Wall. *Independent.*

Ornstein, M. (Director). (2016). *Accidental Courtesy: Daryl Davis, Race & America.*

Lomb, R. (2015). Catching the Dream of the Ute Mountain Ute Tribe—A Glimmer of Hope in a Native 'National Emergency.' *Huffpost.*

Seligman, M. (2006). *Learned Optimism: How to Change Your Mind and Your Life.* Vintage Books.

Oettingen, G. (2015). *Rethinking Positive Thinking: Inside the New Science of Motivation.* Penguin Random House LLC

Oettingen, G., Sevincer, A. T. (2018). *The Psychology of Thinking About the Future.* The Guilford Press.

Echeverria, R. *Four Basic Moods About Life.* Newfield Network Coach Training, 2009-201

Chapter 5: Inspiration – The Energy for Mobilizing

Zenger, J., Folkman, J., Edinger, S. (2009). *The Inspiring Leader: Unlocking The Secrets Of How Extraordinary Leaders Motivate.* McGraw-Hill.

Oleynick, V., Thrash, T., LeFew, M., Moldovan, E., Kieffaber, P. (2014). The scientific study of inspiration in the creative process: challenges and opportunities. *Frontiers in Human Neuroscience.*

Corporate Leadership Council. (2004). Driving Performance and Retention Through Employee Engagement: A Quantitative Analysis of Effective Engagement Strategies. Corporate Executive Board.

Kaufmann, S. B. (2011). Why Inspiration Matters. *Harvard Business Review.*

Folkman, J. (2013). Everything Counts: Six Ways to Inspire and Motivate Top Performance. *Forbes.*

Sinek, S. (2009). How Great Leaders Inspire Action. TEDx Puget Sound.

Mandela, N. (1995). *Long Walk to Freedom: The Autobiography of Nelson Mandela.* Back Bay Books/Little Brown and Company.

Chapter 6: Trust – The Fuel for Collaborating

Fuehrer, C. (2008). *Und wir sind dabei gewesen, Die Revolution, die aus der Kirche kam.* Ullstein Buchverlag GmbH.

Patterson, T. (2009). Europe's Revolution: The pastor who brought down the Berlin Wall. *Independent.*

Covey, S.M.R., Conant, D. R. (2016). The Connection Between Employee Trust and Financial Performance. *Harvard Business Review.*

Taubman, W. (2018). *Gorbachev, His Life and Times.* W.W. Norton & Company Inc.

Feltman, C. (2021) *The Thin Book of® Trust: An Essential Primer for Building Trust at Work, 2nd Edition.* Thin Book Publishing Co.

Khoury, G., Crabtree, S. (2019). Are Businesses Worldwide Suffering from a Trust Crisis? *Gallup.*

Ornstein, M. (Director). (2016). *Accidental Courtesy: Daryl Davis, Race & America.*

Sahadi, J. (2019). Up to Half of Exiting CEOs Don't Quit. They Get Fired. *CCN Business.*

Zak, P. J. (2017). *Trust Factor: The Science of Creating High-Performance Companies.* AMACOM.

Sandahl, P., Phillips, A. (2019). *Teams Unleashed: How To Release the Power and Human Potential of Work Teams.* Nicholas Brealey Publishing.

Lencioni, P. (2002). *The Five Dysfunctions of a Team.* Jossey-Bass.

Chapter 7: Positivity – Being Resilient

Patterson, T. (2009) Europe's Revolution: The pastor who brought down the Berlin Wall. *Independent.*

Fuehrer, C. (2008). *Und wir sind dabei gewesen, Die Revolution, die aus der Kirche kam.* Ullstein Buchverlag GmbH.

Frederickson, B. L., Ph.D. (2009). *Positivity: Top-Notch Research Reveals the Upward Spiral That Will Change Your Life.* Three Rivers Press.

Frederickson, B. L., Ph.D. (2013). *LOVE 2.0, Creating Happiness and Health in Moments of Connection.* Penguin Group.

Brown, B. (2018). *Dare to Lead: Brave Work. Tough Conversations. Whole Hearts.* Vermillions, an imprint of Ebury Publishing.

Sanderson, M.T. (2017). *Symphony For The City Of The Dead.* Candlewick Press.

Ovans, A. (2015). What Resilience Means, and Why It Matters. *Harvard Business Review.*

Grenny, J. (2019). How to Be Resilient in the Face of Harsh Criticism. *Harvard Business Review Press.*

Achor, S., Gielan, M. (2017). Resilience Is About How You Recharge, Not How You Endure. *Harvard Business Review Press.*

Couto, D. (2017). How Resilience Works. *Harvard Business Review Press.*

Frankl, Viktor E. (2006). *Man's Search for Meaning.* Beacon Press.

Lomb, Reiner. (2014). *The Boomerang Approach: Return to Purpose. Ignite Your Passion.*

Sonnenfeld, J. A., Ward, A. J. (2017). Firing Back: How Great Leaders Rebound After Career Disasters. *Harvard Business Review Press.*

Conclusion

Maslow, A. H. (1976). *The Farther Reaches of Human Nature.* Penguin Compass.

Kofman, F. (2018). *The Meaning Revolution – The Power of Transcendent Leadership.* Currency.

Appendix: Applying the Seven Competencies with Other Leadership Models

Blanchard, K. (2007). *Leading at a Higher Level.* Pearson Prentice Hall.

Cameron, K. S., Quinn, R. E. (2011). *Diagnosing and Changing Organizational Culture.* Jossey-Bass.

Jatar, U. (2013). The 7 Disciplines for Building a Transcendent Brand. TEDx Talk.
https://www.youtube.com/watch?v=xS2B1C_xfSg.

About the Author

Reiner is the founder of BoomerangCoach, an executive coaching firm specializing in leadership and career development, innovation, and transformational change. Reiner's mission is to mobilize and develop leaders to create a more sustainable and positive future for all. As an executive coach, he works with leaders and changemakers in a wide range of organizations, from start-ups and multinational companies to non-profits and local communities—all who aspire to create transformational change. Whether he's working with corporate executives, entrepreneurs, intrapreneurs, or indigenous tribal leaders, Reiner's clients appreciate his international business and cross-cultural leadership experience.

Before becoming an executive coach, Reiner had a 30-plus year career in technology, started and developed software businesses, and led leadership development. At Hewlett-Packard, his home for 20-plus years, he launched new software product businesses and helped grow HP Software into a multi-billion dollar organization. While at HP, Reiner discovered his passion and talent in leadership development where he trained leaders in how to scale from leading one's self, to leading others, to leading an entire organization.

Reiner grew up in the western part of a divided Germany during the Cold War. Reiner's heartache over his country's role in the

Holocaust and World War II awoke in him a lifelong desire to address the challenges that threaten future generations.

Reiner is fluent in English and German, and his clients benefit from his global education, deep expertise in sustainability, and his many years as a community organizer. He holds an MBA in Sustainable Business from Pinchot University (now Presidio University) and a Master's Degree in Computer Science from the University of Paderborn (Germany). He is an accredited Professional Certified Coach (PCC) by the International Coaching Federation (ICF). He is also trained and certified in ontological coaching by Newfield Network and in team coaching by Team Coaching International (TCI).

In addition to *ASPIRE*, Reiner is the author of *The Boomerang Approach: Return to Purpose, Ignite Your Passion*.

He lives with his family in Atlanta and works with leaders and changemakers worldwide.

Become a member of Reiner Lomb's community:

Sign up for Reiner's newsletter
- *reinerlomb.com/news/subscribe*

Connect with Reiner on social media
- LinkedIn: *ReinerLomb*
- Twitter: @ReinerLomb

Share ASPIRE with others
- To order copies of ASPIRE go to: *reinerlomb.com/books*

Contact Reiner
- To ask about Reiner's availability for speaking, coaching or workshops go to: *reinerlomb.com/contact*

Printed in Great Britain
by Amazon

79448853R00150